"In this book, *'When God vetoes your plan'* Miracle gives us a window into the mystery of the ways God uses our circumstances to shape our trust, and our character. In a day where bookstores are filled with self help and recipe theology approaches to life ... This book is refreshing return to celebrating the wonder and mystery of a trust and faith filled relationship with a God who is present and attentive yet unpredictable.

Benjamin Franklin once said, "Most men prefer the calm seas of despotism, to the boisterous sea of liberty." This book will give you a compass, and the encouragement you need to leave the safe harbour of your comfort zone, and set the sails of your heart for a daily adventure with Jesus, the lover of your soul, and the captain of your salvation."

Senior Pastor, Paul Berteig *Timbers Community Church*

"This book *'When God vetoes your plan'* explains beautifully that there are times that our best made plans that we would like God to sanction can be prohibited by the Father (God) for our benefit. It reminds us that God is sovereign over our lives and encourages us to live a life without mediocrity. This book reveals fresh insight that can help every reader to embrace the notion of living life without limits and allowing God's agenda to be the plan from which they navigate their lives to live on purpose. The author uses real-life stories and knowledge to help us learn to embrace God's complete healing for our past disappointments and disarm the lodged memories that holds us captive. An alternative conceptualization of recognizing our beauty, abilities, and uniqueness challenges us to transform our mindset to live freely without boundaries. This book will transform you as you discover personal freedom from your past. This book is an excellent resource for anyone who truly desires to live their best life now and in the future. I highly recommend this book for those seeking insight of God's plans for their lives."

Dr. Nicole R. Baptiste
Author of *'This is your greater year!: A journey of waiting on God's Promises'*
Senior Consultant at 'New Millennium Leadership & Consulting Inc.'

*When God Vetoes Your Plan* is a life-changing and liberating word for every individual that is looking to be set free from the shackles of mediocrity and the pain of their past. This book will give you the courage and support necessary to sit back, and allow God to veto your plan. Miracle…thank you for allowing God to veto yours. The Kingdom is forever grateful!

FranShon Reid, Bethel A.M.E Church<br>
Young Adult Minister & The National Singles Prayer<br>
& Advice Hotline Co-Visionary

In this book, "*When God Vetoes your plans*", Miracle gives us an amazing approach on how sometimes life's transitions can bring forth a divine eye opener for God's plan. We all have dreams and goals for what and where we would like to end up and be in life but that isn't always the plan God has for us. Through personal reflection and testimony Miracle, gives proof of the scripture in 2 Corinthians 5:7, that if you want to have a limitless life you have to walk by faith and not by sight. In this book Miracle shows you that if you truly have faith, letting go of our own agenda and allowing God to guide you, you will truly have a limitless life. I highly recommend this book to all Kingdom Leaders, Worship Leaders, and to all who are serious about Kingdom business.

Frederick J. Dukes Jr.<br>
Christian Recording Artist, Worship Leader, Motivational Speaker

# When God VETOES Your Plan

## AN INVITATION TO A LIFE WITHOUT LIMITS

## MIRACLE REED

WestBow
PRESS
A DIVISION OF THOMAS NELSON

Copyright © 2013 Miracle Reed.

All rights reserved. No part of this book may be used or reproduced by any means, graphic, electronic, or mechanical, including photocopying, recording, taping or by any information storage retrieval system without the written permission of the publisher except in the case of brief quotations embodied in critical articles and reviews.

WestBow Press books may be ordered through booksellers or by contacting:

WestBow Press
A Division of Thomas Nelson
1663 Liberty Drive
Bloomington, IN 47403
www.westbowpress.com
1 (866) 928-1240

Because of the dynamic nature of the Internet, any web addresses or links contained in this book may have changed since publication and may no longer be valid. The views expressed in this work are solely those of the author and do not necessarily reflect the views of the publisher, and the publisher hereby disclaims any responsibility for them.

Any people depicted in stock imagery provided by Thinkstock are models, and such images are being used for illustrative purposes only. Certain stock imagery © Thinkstock.

ISBN: 978-1-4908-1636-4 (sc)
ISBN: 978-1-4908-1637-1 (hc)
ISBN: 978-1-4908-1635-7 (e)

Library of Congress Control Number: 2013921401

Printed in the United States of America.

WestBow Press rev. date: 12/4/2013

# Dedication

I dedicate this book to my beginning (Pittsburgh, Pa),
my journey (St.Croix, USVI),
my present (Prince George, BC, Canada)
and to the future plan of God.

# CONTENTS

Endorsements ................................................................. i
Foreword- Mark James ................................................ ix
Introduction ................................................................. xi

Chapter 1    Just Say Yes ............................................... 1
Chapter 2    No More Snacks ........................................ 5
Chapter 3    What You Feed Will Grow; What You Starve
             Will Die ................................................... 11
Chapter 4    The Privileged Life .................................. 15
Chapter 5    Orchid ..................................................... 20
Chapter 6    Resume Number 29 ................................ 25
Chapter 7    Plans Change .......................................... 29
Chapter 8    The Give-Up and the Gain ..................... 34
Chapter 9    Bounce Back ........................................... 38
Chapter 10   Go with the Flow ................................... 47
Chapter 11   Oh, Canada ............................................ 50
Chapter 12   The Lie of Limit in the Midst of Abundance ............ 57
Chapter 13   Walks in the Park .................................. 60
Chapter 14   Sink or Swim ......................................... 64
Chapter 15   Pack Light .............................................. 67
Chapter 16   Carry On ................................................ 69
Chapter 17   Fear Came Knocking ............................. 73
Chapter 18   The Journey ........................................... 76
Chapter 19   This Is Temporary ................................. 84
Chapter 20   Ms. Independent .................................... 89

Chapter 21  Life of Freedom ........................................................... 94
Chapter 22  I Don't Want to Go to Sleep ...................................... 100
Chapter 23  How Did It All Start? ................................................. 103
Chapter 24  You Only Get One ..................................................... 106
Chapter 25  Happily Ever After ..................................................... 109

Epilogue ............................................................................................. 111
Thoughts ............................................................................................ 113
About the Author ............................................................................. 119

# FOREWORD

Miracle Reed is a messenger for our generation. From the time I was first introduced to her as a vibrant pre-teen, it was clear to me that she had a deliberate intention toward God and that His anointing was upon her life. The words "deliberate intention" are critical because as a young person, her entire being (mind, body and spirit) were clearly and consistently directed toward serving God. There was no confusion. There was no inconsistency from her. There was no miscalculation. We all knew she was of God and for God. It was clear to me that Miracle had been given a mandate - the purpose of which had not been revealed to me just yet. Strangely, I knew I was meant to be intertwined in her journey. Later, when I became married, my wife felt the same conviction. Today we think of her as another daughter within our family and I am proud to mentor her as God so allows.

Miracle's message and style is void of the template jargon and literary vibrato that pervades Christian literature today. She is personable in a way that allows you to connect with certain people. Readers will discover a new sound and a new vibration in her writing that will reorient their paradigms of how we respond to God. As you discover these new paradigms, you will be astonished as to how they teach you to find new manna within the catacombs of your life that were written off as dead and not worth reviving. I'm talking about new discoveries in the previously traversed areas of your life… similar to finding a secret passage within an old house you grew up in. I love reality shows about mining and archaeology so I will use the analogy of unearthing gold within an area that you (and others) had already mined years ago and now considered exhausted. Imagine your thrill when everyone told you that your efforts would be a waste of time, but you were bold enough to revisit these supposedly barren lands… and struck gold!!!

Miracle's message represents an invitation to break free from the self-imposed limits we experience in our journey with God. It is NOT an invitation to think and live outside the box. Rather, it is an an expression of God's permission to live WITHOUT THE BOX! It is a road map designed to release us from the constraints of rigid expectations by teaching us to re-evaluate our response when life doesn't happen as planned. Miracle Reed gives us permission and the process needed to make us more available for God.

What excites me about this book is the spiritual multiplier effect that it will have within the Kingdom of God. You will not evaluate your life's experiences the same way after reading. Equally exciting is what I know will be found by each reader who is seeking a deeper connection with God. It can be summed up in one word… "Access". The author has provided a number of prescriptions for helping God's children reclaim their access to Him. Not the concert access you might akin to seeing an entertainer perform on-stage, but more like a private dinner and discussion with that artist while they were creating the music. I'm talking about actually seeing the artistry unfold before your eyes and understanding the artist's intention behind it. Miracle gives us permission to find, see and know our Heavenly Father outside of the traditional boundaries we are so use to. This is a message for our time and well worth the read.

My prayer for the reader, is that as you read this book please give yourself permission to take just a little risk and stray away from another day of normalcy. Regardless of your age, race, economic status or current condition in life, I hope that you will make today the day that you wander back to an old garden you have already harvested, and find new fruit therein. Be blessed.

Mark James

# INTRODUCTION

*When God Vetoes Your Plan*

As a teenager, I planned my entire life. I would live in the Maryland/DC area, hold a master of divinity from Howard University, travel the world as a preacher, and more than likely, marry in my early twenties. However, I currently live in British Columbia, Canada. I have received two bachelor degrees from Geneva College, located in Western Pennsylvania, and I have never been married or engaged. Furthermore, my plan was limited to what I thought would bring some level of joy, achievement, love, and acceptance. My plan was clearly vetoed by God, and for that I am truly thankful.

It wasn't until a ministry opportunity opened for me in St. Croix (in the US Virgin Islands) back in 2008 that I really began to understand the meaning of God's plan. I never planned to live in the Caribbean and become forever changed as a result of it, but God did. I never thought in a million years that I would experience such wealth in meeting people from all over the world, but God did. I definitely never thought that I would write a book while living in St. Croix or Canada, but God sure did.

The whole time, God tried to invite me to a life that was without limits. You know the kind of life that you convince yourself is for someone else—a life that seems unattainable? I also used to think that a life without limits would be nearly impossible. I imagined that I would have to do certain things, obtain certain degrees, become a wife, and accomplish great feats to believe that I had a life of fulfillment.

However, once I began to seek understanding concerning what it means to live a life without limits, I learned that this life would require less of me and more of God. This life would also require me to fully embrace who God is and believe with all of my heart that everything He has for me is good. Yes, everything. You may think, *How could one possibly believe that everything God has for him or her is good when the person has experienced such turmoil?* This is a valid question that I had to explore myself. I realized that my perception of God and His capabilities was incorrect. Just like you, I allowed myself to become bombarded by negativity instead of giving life a chance to surprise me. In life, there are occurrences when the presence of evil is visible. But being that good always wins in the end, the focus and attention must not be placed on what seems to be wrong now but what will be right later.

Understanding the role that God has in your life and the world is a defining factor in realizing how limited you are or how limited you allow yourself to become as a result of it. Many of your plans have already been vetoed by God; hence the fact that you are still waiting. However, I invite you to become free from those plans that have been vetoed and accept a life that will far exceed anything that you could imagine.

I've made quite a few plans over the years and created the famous five-year plan as well, hoping that in some way, God would possibly cosign them—but He didn't. I recognized that God had vetoed my plans and that I was invited to live a life that would exceed my expectations and take me far beyond the limitations that are often created when plans are made. I invite you to come along this lifetime journey of living a life without limits that welcomes less of ourselves and more of God—a life that that is free from the limitations created by your plans.

# CHAPTER 1

## Just Say Yes

*I used to think that God expected a lot from me, and then I realized that I didn't have anything to give Him.*

Have you ever felt extremely burdened by the idea of God wanting something from you? Yeah, me too. Sometimes I think, *God, I don't think I have what it takes. I don't have the time, money, education, or resources to do what you want me to do. So please just pick someone else.* Then it hits me! God couldn't possibly want anything from us. You don't have anything to give Him—and if that's the case, He must want to do something with you. I have often felt that I didn't quite make the cut or have what it took. However, I've learned over the years that the only limit in life is that which has been created by self.

There are no limits to the possibilities of what you can accomplish in this life. However, limits can be created from a lack of understanding personal worth and value. Your lack of understanding who you are can be a detriment to every aspect of your life. Not knowing who you are can keep you in a job you hate, relationship you despise, or house you can't afford. This is not the life you have been created to live. However, many make this life a reality by choice. But you have the ability to stop this negative cycle in your life today.

Show me someone who thinks he or she can do anything, and I will show you someone who acknowledges that his or her strengths and talents are gifts. Do you know that you can actually talk yourself out of greatness by what you feed yourself mentally? Have you ever met a person who was externally gorgeous but constantly complained about how he or she looked? Have you had a coworker who was up for promotion but continually talked down about his or her performance? How is it that others can encourage, promote, and believe in us, but we can't see what they see for ourselves? I believe the answer is rooted in lies that we've believed the majority of our lives. No matter how successful we become, all we continually see are those lies.

Experiences have a major impact on how we view ourselves, others, and God. Based on those experiences—whether good or bad—a person will either choose to be in a favor of himself or herself, others, and God or not. However, if a person is hurt in a church setting or judged by someone who claims to be Christian, chances are that they would not be in a favor of any religious setting. This gives clear insight into what we allow ourselves to be influenced by. As you read this chapter, ask yourself, "Did I say yes to God? Did I say yes to myself, or have I tried to work my way to where I think I should be at this point in life?"

As I prepared to graduate from high school, a challenging situation occurred. I had received a rejection letter from the only college that I had applied to, Geneva. I felt overwhelmed and distraught by what this could mean for my future plans. I went to my guidance counselor and shared with her what happened and that they asked me to retake the SATs. She said not to worry about it—but how could I not? It was the only school that I had applied to, and the thought of not getting accepted had never crossed my mind. I had been an honor roll student my entire life, volunteered in countless hours of community service, and was a minister.

I thought to myself, *How could this happen to me?* Little did I know that God was up to a master plan that would completely exceed all of my hopes. A few weeks later, without retaking the SAT, I received an acceptance letter from Geneva. I was in shock and couldn't believe it. I wondered how in the world this could happen. So I went back to my guidance counselor, and what I was getting ready to hear, would blow me away.

My guidance counselor told me that she called the school and spoke to the Dean of Admissions. She told the Dean all about me, what an asset I was to my high school, and the asset I would be to Geneva College. I can only imagine what the Dean said to her after she finished promoting me. However, I do know that ultimately, he said, "Yes, she's in." The amazing thing is not that I was accepted into the program on her word as much as the fact that I was accepted with over 80 percent of my tuition covered—not with loans, but by scholarships and state grants. The other challenge of attending a school such as Geneva was the six-figure price that came packaged with the acceptance letter. My family certainly could not afford it, but we believed that if God got me into the school, He would see to it that it was paid for. And He certainly did! To this day, I am still amazed by God's favor in my life.

I am led to believe without any other choice that I am no different from you. I can say that because I have many friends in my life who have seen the blessings of God come out of nowhere. The correlation between all of us has been our "Yes" answers to the extended invitation to live life without limits. It certainly has nothing to do with where you come from, who your parents are, or if you were raised in a religious family. It's about your answer to God's invitation. The life that awaits you is not being held up by your finances, divorce, unemployment, or children; it is being held up by your delay in responding with a selfless yes, in the words of Stanley Hopkins. I say selfless, because this life will require less of you and more of "Him" (God).

Don't worry about what other people may think or say as a result of your acceptance of this invitation. Invite them along for the journey as well! They certainly will not be disappointed. Just as you will be in for a shock once entering into this new life, so will they. I can guarantee that they will thank you for it. They will even wonder what took you so long to extend the invitation. They will have questions, just like you, but keep in mind that this invitation is

God's way of reeling you in to do something with Him and not for Him. God gives you the esteemed privilege of living a life without limits with Him.

Every decision you make now can either bring you closer to this life, or draw you further from it. You have a daily decision to make. The life that you are invited to live is a daily decision to choose what is great, not just what is good. It's having the ability and privilege to wake up each day filled with joy because of all that life has to offer. Can you imagine waking up thinking of the endless possibilities of what each day could bring? This could be your life! Every decision that you make now sets you up for a place of favor.

I had no idea that my acceptance to Geneva College would be based on the life that I had lived up to that point, but it was. Everything that I did prior to entering the bachelor's program would play a major role in my acceptance. In fact, if it had not been for my "Yes" to God's invitation way back then, the "No" that Geneva gave initially would have remained. I encourage you to stay motivated in what you are doing, even if it seems to go unnoticed. At the proper time, your work will be rewarded, and the response that used to be "No" will soon turn into a "Yes."

# CHAPTER 2

## No More Snacks

*Have you ever had a snack that tasted so good, it made your forget that you were waiting on the main course?*

I absolutely love sweets. In fact, I could live off cupcakes alone. When I go away on vacation, one of the first things that I do is go to the bakery that is said to be the best in town. I just love a good dessert. I live in a small city called Prince George in northern BC, and when I learned that there was a restaurant here that had white chocolate mousse cake and a cupcakery that was a three-minute walk from my office, I could have floated on air. It was like music to my ears.

Once I began to indulge in the amazing goodies that were made available to me daily, my appetite and cravings started to change. I no longer had the hankering that I once had. I snacked so much that not only did my appetite for food decrease, but also my appetite for what I once enjoyed every day. The dessert in the beginning of my day, afternoon, or evening caused me to lose sight of the fact that I had no desire to eat dinner because I allowed myself to become full off of three or four cupcakes! I know that sounds intense, but it's the truth. Sometimes I even had five. I know it's horrible, but don't judge me. I am no longer the same—trust me. I've learned to say, "No more snacks today."

However, it's unfortunate that some of us will live our lives this way, unable to say no to artificial fillers in different areas. We will indulge in things that satisfy our desires temporarily. In this way, we cheat ourselves. It's almost as if we live for the day or moment—as if that which we desire will run out or no longer be made available. It may have something to do with a lack of balance with that which is healthy and that which is an occasional treat. If you never take the time to enjoy the balance of both, it can become quite a detriment to the life you were created to have.

The reason I indulged in dessert the way that I did was because I had an "I just can't get enough" mentality. This mentality, nine times out of ten, leads to nothing positive, whether it is about food, relationships, or money. The fact that God vetoes our plans is a clear indicator that most of the time, we are unaware of the unforeseen harm that will take place at some point.

As a single woman, I often asked God if marriage was a part of the plan, but then I realized that the response didn't matter. At the moment I said, "No more snacks," I decided to not limit that to dessert (because my life has no limits), but also my emotional availability for a relationship. This does not mean that I am not open to the possibility of someday being married; I welcome it. However, during this season of my life, that level of availability is on reserve. I am content and filled with joy as a result. This chapter will begin to hit home for some married and single people.

Our indulgent cravings are not limited to what we eat; in fact, some won't be able to relate to the dessert indulgent cravings. However, this does not mean that there are no snacks in your life. It just means that your snack may be a bit more discreet. Perhaps you are like me, determined to only be in a relationship that exemplifies your personal view of your own worth and value. Perhaps you have been single for a while by choice, but you allow people into your mental space by making your time available to them, only to find out that they were either using you as a snack or you had allowed them to become a snack in your life. This happens quicker and more subtly than one can imagine.

Anything or anyone that you allow into your life has the potential of either helping you grow because he or she possesses natural abilities to do so, or helping you indulge in that which can only artificially satisfy for your craving. This is not something that you can bring out of another; it is a natural ability that one possesses as a gift or because of the way in which he or she was raised. Too often, we try to help a person be who and what we think he or she should be when in actuality, that person either doesn't see it for himself or herself or doesn't want it. This was revealed to me concerning decisions I made. My eyes were really opened!

I have met many people who had a lot going for them and were easy on the eyes. But it didn't take long for me to see that there was no possibility of anything more than casual conversations here and there. However, I continued to snack on the nonexistent possibility. This led me to the realization that what I did with my desserts, I also did by allowing myself to become emotionally available to nonexistent potential. In the same way I indulged in desserts, creating a lack of hunger or appetite for the main course that was being prepared, I allowed myself to carry on conversations with people who I knew had no potential to be my life partner.

The interesting thing about this concept in reference to making oneself available emotionally is that the emotional attachment acts as a filler—just a junk food or dessert. I have met some amazing people along the way. However, I allowed some of them to occupy a space in my life that created a lack of availability to receive what God may have for me in the long run, because I was artificially full of their sweetness. We are all guilty—at some point or another—of saying, "Well, maybe ..." in reference to what could possibly change our initial "This isn't him or her" response.

The key to understanding this process is being able to be honest with yourself concerning your thoughts and feelings. I have found in counseling both married and single people that most decisions are based on a place of vulnerability, lack of trust, insecurity, or loneliness that has not been confidentially shared with one who can be trusted. Everyday concerns remain unspoken; there becomes an unstable bridge that is bound to collapse.

The fact that I committed to no longer snack in the context of emotional availability gave me freedom from ever thinking of what should have been done or said differently. I was not always able to say that, but at this point, I realize that living a life without limits removes the risk of me getting in the way. Have you ever thought to yourself after making a decision, *What was I thinking?* and then answered your own question with, *I wasn't; that's the problem?* If so, this alone proves the fact that many times, we tend to get in our own way. Furthermore, we tend to not have a solution as to how we are going to get out of it, and then we end up feeling guilty. This is not the invitation that is given to you.

On the contrary, life without limits offers you the ability to be free from yourself and making attempts to figure out a solution for every problem that comes your way. You become free from limits because you become free from yourself. A life without limits means a life that welcomes less of you and more of Him. This is not an easy process. It is never easy to let go of what is routine. However, once you let your plan go and welcome a new life, this process will become much easier.

You may think, *So, does this invitation really mean that I don't have to make any decisions?* Yes, that is exactly what I am saying. However, don't be misled; a lack of decision-making does not mean a lack of responsibility and accountability for one's actions. The life that you welcome will require you to let go of what you think is for you and what you think is not for you. That mind-set alone is limited, not to mention the actions and lifestyle that come along with it. Let's begin this journey by taking a moment and jotting down a few things. (Don't worry. This is not for you to give to anyone; this is a private exercise for you.)

Go to the Thoughts section at the end of the book. Write down where you currently are financially (in debt, financially free, or on the way to financial freedom), relationally (married, single, divorced, widowed, broken, etc.), emotionally (depressed, stressed, suicidal, encouraged, burdened, excited, etc.), spiritually (religious, undecided, seeking/exploring, etc.), and confidently (high, low, non-existent, seasonal, etc.).

After you take some time to jot down your response, write over your response in big, bold letters, **"Limited."** The response that you just gave for this brief exercise allows you to visualize how you have allowed your state of mind and everything else to identify you, discourage you, encourage you, become a lie that you live, or even become a fear that you have fed. Stop doing that to yourself. You will never be identified by what you have or the experiences that have tainted your outlook on life. Let's move past those roles, titles, and feelings and say, "No more snacks." It is now time to feed yourself that which will bring forth growth rather than welcoming situations, people, or self-doubt that will stunt your growth.

Maybe you never felt like you had worth or value outside of a relationship. Maybe you have lived your entire life in the shadows of what other people thought about you. Maybe you have allowed yourself to snack for years, and at this point, you realize that you have neglected everything and everyone that could add substance to your life. Well, if you have, stop. You are much better than what you think and worth more than "the" amount of men or women whose attention you can draw. Those are artificial tools that have been used to keep you stuck. Quite frankly, you should be tired of always feeling empty and reaching goals that were created out of frustration, hurt, and rejection. It's time to give all of that up. A feast awaits you.

Almost everything you've tried has failed, so why not try something that requires less of you? The relationship didn't work, your job drains you every day, your parenting skills could use some help, and the amount of debt that you've racked while trying to keep up with the Jones' has left your depleted of all disposable income. It's time to place it all in God's hands. Stop trying to fight what is clearly defeating you. I know you've been raised to never throw in the towel, but when you throw it into the hands of God, it becomes a gain, not a give-up!

You may feel like so many of your plans were vetoed by God that you've lost your motivation to plan again. Accepting this invitation to live a life without limits means living a life without plans! In fact, it's a good thing that your plans were vetoed. Can you imagine where you would be today if you stayed at that miserable job, still took those antidepressants despite the side effects, and or stayed in the relationship that stripped you of all dignity? Life would have been extremely limited; you would not be able to actually classify it as living. You must understand who you are and what you were created to become.

My plan was small and limited in comparison to what God has done—what a snack that would have been! Life was not meant to be limited to what we can do or have been naturally gifted to accomplish. Life was meant to be full of surprises, twists, and turns that keep you on the edge of your seat, waiting for what's next, not bored by the routine that was created. It's time to live! Don't allow yourself to spend another day snacking on that which is temporary when you were created to feast off life. Say, "No more snacks."

# CHAPTER 3

# What You Feed Will Grow; What You Starve Will Die

*Life is about being intoxicated by the beauty of every season you find yourself in.*

There are no defining factors in understanding the ways of God. In fact, the Bible mentions the incapability of humans even trying to understand the ways of God. However, God knows what He is doing even when we don't. As you accept the invitation to live a life without limits, you are also encouraged to not waste another day trying to figure God out. It is exhausting and in no way your job or duty. Furthermore, it takes your attention off the facts. If you no longer live your life according to your plans, then there is nothing left for you to figure out. You live by faith, believing that there is a God who holds your life in His hands and calls for you to trust Him.

You've made the decision to live a life without artificial fillers, or snacks, so now it is time to consider the other areas of your life that you may be feeding. Maybe you have felt limited because of things that you didn't have as a child. Maybe your father wasn't around or your mother was too busy taking care of your younger siblings, so you were left to fend for yourself. Maybe you never heard your father tell you that you were a man, and as a result, you've struggled with knowing who you really are. Only you know the situations that cause you to think less of yourself. The more you feed yourself negative thoughts and what televangelist Joyce Meyers classifies as "stinking thinking," the more your life will be permeated with seeds of doubt and death.

There comes a time in everyone's life when self-inventory must take place. This is a needed process for growth and also for personal inventory of things in your life that may be dying, need to grow, and are growing but need to die. We can sometimes make the mistake of feeding that which needs to die and killing that which needs to live. These can include mind-sets, ways of life, forgiveness, moving on, or maybe even forgetting. Make time to take an introspective look at the brief exercise that you did in chapter 2, and think of some of the areas that need to expand or decrease.

For a period in my life, I felt extremely low about myself. Though no one would ever be able to tell because of my expertise in hiding it, it was clear and present before me. I knew I had allowed lies to take root in my life, and I continued to feed them based on my actions. Whether or not people know what you are going through, the key principle to freedom is being able to be honest with yourself. I came to a place in my life where I did not like what I saw when I looked in the mirror. I wore tons of makeup and felt like my looks were never good enough. I could hide behind a false sense of confidence, but all the while, I wished I looked completely different.

However, as I look back over that season of my life, I recognize that most of my insecurities came from looking at the appearance of others. It is easy to become stuck on what other people have when you don't realize what you have. This is why God vetoes your plan and goals of attainment. He knows that you look for those things to identify you. Maybe you spent your life, hoping and praying that the new job, house, or car would make you feel better rather than allowing God to remove the false ideals that have been created concerning gain. You were created to be great; the key is actually believing it. When I actually started believing that I had the ability to change my environment and be a bridge of hope for people, my life changed, and the way that I viewed myself changed as well. When you begin to believe in what you are capable of, you will begin to look at your life in a different way.

You may ask, "Well, Miracle, how do I begin to rid my life of that which needs to die, and how do I welcome the things that I need in my life?" Start by looking at your list from the previous chapter and ask yourself, "Have I allowed any of these roles or areas of my life to identify my worth or value? Have I allowed people to discredit me as a result of those specific areas? Have I disqualified myself based on where I stand in those areas?" This series of questions can be used as a starting point because your responses will help you to identify the lies that you have fed yourself. All lies must die, no matter how long you have lived with them. No matter who convinced you of them, they need to go.

**Here is a daily declaration that will serve as tool of spiritual empowerment:**

> I declare my current status in finances, relationships, emotional stability, employment, or family do not identify who I am but are roles that I carry in this life. I will no longer make plans, hoping that God will cosign them; I will trust His plan for my life. I am not held back or held down by any decisions that I've made in my past, because the only relevance my past has is that which I give. I consider it an honor that God vetoed my plan because it was too small, limited, and tailored to the lies that I've believed concerning success and fulfillment.
>
> I am determined to live a life without limits, and I acknowledge that this new way of living will require me to let go of myself. I may have days when this is a challenge, but I will not be moved or deterred from the life that has been created for me. At this very moment, I

release myself from the box that I've lived in and take my place in a life without limits.

I have no idea where this life will take me, but I trust that everything God has for me is good and the situations that do not seem in my favor will turn out to be part of His plan for my life that ultimately will work out for my good. I refuse to feed myself trash when I am destined to eat only the finest. I refuse to go another day without being intoxicated by the beauty of every season in which I find myself. I accept the invitation. This is my life—a life without limits.

# CHAPTER 4

## The Privileged Life

*I thought wealth allowed one to live the privileged life. Then I realized that there are some who have financial wealth but live the life of a pauper. Wealth is a state of mind.*

My family, in the standards of the world, was not rich by any means. Although my grandma drove a black 1989 Fleetwood Cadillac during my childhood, made sure that I was enrolled in private school my entire life, and ensured I had the best of everything, we still didn't quite make the cut for financial wealth. The Pittsburgh neighborhood that I grew up in and still call home would definitely be considered the city. However, the interesting dynamic to our neighborhood, which is now inner-city, didn't start off that way. My grandmother moved into the area over forty year ago and was considered to be the wealthy one in the family due to the standards of the neighborhood as well as the car she drove. That neighborhood was once upscale—but just like various aspects of our lives, time changed things.

Our lives are much like the neighborhood that I grew up in. They start out with great prestige and privileges, but somewhere down the line, we allow people to come in who do not respect or honor our property. This happens easily and becomes a common thread in the lives of many people. We set out with goals and create high standards for ourselves, but somewhere down the line, we allow people to encourage, manipulate, and even control us to the point of changing our once high-class standards to lives of limitation. Your life that was once bright and full of dreams and aspirations quickly became shattered. Much like the neighborhood, over time, people moved in who had no clue of what it used to be and could care less for its maintenance. However, at Grandma's house, there was a sense of peace, beauty, and grace. The foundation of what used to be remained at her house.

At the age of fifteen, I started a youth ministry right in my grandmother's home called Generation for Christ. It became so influential that I received invites to minister on television and share the vision behind the youth ministry. Reporters even came to the house during a session to write an article about it. Youth from various parts of the city came, and parents were amazed that their children stayed at someone's house until 2:00 or 3:00 a.m. reading the Bible and spending time in worship with God.

My grandmother cooked every Friday as well, which possibly became the motivation for some. I can't blame them, though; my grandmother makes some mean fried chicken. I believe God has blessed grandmothers to all be amazing cooks! It's awesome how that works. My grandmother also baked a cake along with the other food items for the night. We created a family—an environment that was closed off and secure from all that went on around us. A piece of the foundation that was once our neighborhood became our home.

I ministered to the drug dealers in the neighborhood on multiple occasions in the same church parking lot where all sorts of nonsense took place. Before I became a teenager, I began to understand that I had something in my life that I wanted everyone else to have as well. It was a life of privilege that could change a person and the things around him or her. I felt like the life I had was too good to keep to myself, so I began a mission to evangelize to my neighborhood! And I actually did. Every drug dealer in the area referred to me as "Miracle, the little preacher."

## WHEN GOD VETOES YOUR PLAN

On one particular day, I gained enough boldness and courage to walk over to the church parking lot and offer a word of prayer. I was about twelve years old, walking over to a parking lot full of luxury cars, bass systems that caused the whole block to shake, and men smoking blunts hanging out the side of their cars. There were women there as well. I was actually a bit nervous, so as I walked over, I had one of the guys get the crew's attention. He yelled above the music, "Ayo, get out the cars. Li'l Miracle wants to pray with us."

At first, there was no movement, but then he yelled once more, "Ayo, I said get out the cars; she trynna' pray with us." At that point, all of the men got out of their cars, turned their music off, put away what they were smoking, linked up in a circle, and allowed me to pray with them. This was the beginning of my life being vetoed by God for the sake of those who've been overlooked.

That day changed my view of the possibilities that I had in life. This experience opened my eyes to see that if you have something that has changed your life, there is a chance that it can change others' lives as well. Allow the concept of the privileged life to connect with you to the point that limits and preconceived notions are removed. The ideas that you once had concerning having a privileged life were limited to it being a state of being, not a state of mind. You may be unemployed, divorced, or paralyzed, but your state of mind moves you from a place of being to a place of living in purpose.

The invitation that is extended to you and me is one that changes and transforms the way we think and view life. You have the choice to continually live in what has happened to you or to live in what you can make happen for yourself. This is progressive and processional thinking. It does not happen overnight, but it does begin at the moment you decide to make it your life. This comes by understanding that God coming in your life and vetoing your plans was all a setup. That's right; He set you up to do something far greater than what you could have ever imagined. The choice is yours.

I had a choice as to whether or not I would accept the invitation as well. An invitation was made to grow, live, and experience love from an amazing group of people in Canada who I now consider family. I could have said no due to a mind-set of limitations, or I could accept the offer, realizing that my life is not my own.

I have been in British Columbia, Canada now for two years, and I would have never imagined that all of this waited on my "Yes." Sometimes we kick and scream our way out of seasons of blessings and don't even know it. We allow the fear of the unknown to keep us from some great opportunities, relationships, vacation plans, and adventures. Furthermore, we become limited even in our way of experiencing life.

Refuse to accept a limited experience in life. You have been created for much more than what you could ever imagine. Don't stay stuck because you can't find people to go with you. Just go. There are people assigned to you along the way, but you must first pick up your feet and start moving.

We live in a society in which the possibility of reaching thousands and even millions of people lies right in front of our screens. Whether through your television, telephone, or computer, you have the ability to send out whatever message you choose when you decide. Does the fact that you have survived all that you've been through trigger any type of motivation to inspire others with all of the access that you have? I came to the conclusion some time ago that my life story was worth hearing. In fact, I became crazy enough to believe that I live such a privileged life and had such an amazing and challenging journey that other people needed to hear it. I believe that our lives can become bridges of hope for those whose bridges have collapsed.

This is the privileged life that I extend to you. I welcome you to all that it has to offer. It is a life without limits, a life of hope, a life that inspires, a life that does not take no for an answer, and a life that is not moved by a neighborhood that has seen better days. I invite you to a life that can change everything you have and everything you have become for the better. It's time to step out of a place of complacency and get moving!

You have the ability to write a blog, write a book, create a YouTube channel, and have followers from multiple social networking sites—and a vast number of possibilities for where it could go from there. Your voice needs to be heard. Your life is a bridge of hope to someone, and you don't need financial wealth to gain access to be that bridge. "You don't have to be rich to make things happen; you just need people around you who believe in you and are willing to invest in what you are doing."

There are more people in our world than we think who are waiting for creative and innovative ideas to invest in. The challenge that lies within all of us is believing in ourselves enough to step out and take action. It doesn't matter where you come from, what you currently have, or what people have said about you. What matters is that you believe you can do something. This is what happens when God vetoes your plan; He invites you to a life without limits.

# CHAPTER 5

## Orchid

*I don't believe in payments. I believe in having what is needed or waiting until you do.*

When I moved to Canada, I was without a vehicle. I was determined that I would not go into debt by purchasing a vehicle that would need payments, so I was willing to wait it out. Many people said that they knew people who could give me a deal, but my mind was made up. I was not willing to make payments on a vehicle. Contrary to the way our society works, I did not want to get something immediately and pay later.

At the age of eighteen, I thought I was an adult, so I purchased a very expensive cell phone that incurred thousands of dollars in charges, applied for multiple department store cards that quickly became maxed out, and got a Chase card that was offered right before I went away to Geneva. Needless to say, I developed a fair share of debt. However, a few years later, I was able to pay everything off. I understood that if I still had a mind-set of debt, I would at some point find myself in the same trap, and I was determined to no longer live that life.

On June 5, 2011, I sat in a church service in Greensboro, North Carolina—Evangel Fellowship under the leadership of the late Bishop Otis Lockett. He preached a message titled "Continual Increase

Blessings". He passionately ministered from the perspective of being financially free and not being bound to unwise decisions made concerning money. He said that we all have the ability to be free financially and live out biblical principles concerning the privileges that God has for us.

In that moment, I knew that God was talking directly to me. I sat in the front row with First Lady Lockett, and the tears began to flow. I heard God speak to me clearly; He asked me if I was done taking financial matters into my own hands. Though I had paid off the debt that had incurred, I still had a shopping problem. It wasn't on credit, but I spent my last to get that new purse, shoes, or whatever else I wanted or thought that I needed at that time. This is not the lifestyle that has been created for those who choose to live life without limits.

A life without limits does not make decisions as if there will never be another time to buy something of interest. In fact, a life without limits is a life that is selective in what is chosen and does not rush or make purchases off of impulse. These kinds of behavior patterns stem from a state of mind that is limited. This state of mind comes from being improperly taught self-control, patience, and contentment. When you understand who you are and what you have access to, you become content in waiting because you know that it's available to you at any given time.

Let's think for a moment of a shopping spree. It is a concept that denotes a limited time when an offer is made available or the ability to buy an excessive amount of items, as if the store is going out of business, which also denotes limitation. When you realize that God vetoed your plan because He had something better, you realize that most of what you want is below the standard of what He has for you. Can we take it a step further and think of dating sprees? Once again, it is a concept that camouflages itself in plenty, but underneath the surface, limitation is found.

You allow yourself to become emotionally and physically available, opening doors that seldom close all the way once they've been opened. What started off as a life of pride due to having multiple persons interested in a pursuit leads to a life masked in insecurity and brokenness. This can be avoided if you so choose. This does not have to be a part of your story. However, if it is, what better way to lead others out of it than to demonstrate the ways in which your eyes were opened and your heart was changed than with your actions? When doors that involve other people are opened, it is imperative that proper time is taken to forgive oneself because there are and will be occasions when people will not be able to get past what they feel concerning you, but you will need to.

The orchid has always been a reflection of perfect timing, being properly positioned, and an indicator of moving on. I absolutely love orchids and consider them to be a display of great beauty. They are strategically placed wherever I go by people who are unaware of my love for them. In many ways, I believe that it's God's way of saying, "Today, you are right where you are supposed to be, and I have placed this symbol of beauty before you as a reminder."

I live close enough to everything to get around on foot, so transportation was not a big deal, especially being that I moved to Canada in the summer. Little did I know that God would use my lack of transportation as a reminder of His beauty and presence in my life.

I had finished teaching young adults, and a couple who was there asked me if I needed a vehicle. I hesitantly responded, "Yes, I do."

Their immediate response was, "Well, we have an extra vehicle; you are welcome to use it whenever you want." I was shocked by their generosity and couldn't help but think, *Wow, God, the people up here in Canada are extremely generous and kind.* But the story gets better. About thirty minutes later, I received a phone call from the husband saying that he and his wife just finished talking about the car, and they felt like God wanted them to give me the car for free!

I said, "No way; you have to be kidding me." A few months prior to moving to Canada, I talked with my grandma and shared that if I could buy any car without a car payment outside of my favorite car (a black Audi), it would be a Volkswagen. She was the only one who knew about my new car interest. While I felt overwhelmed with excitement and joy, the couple asked me over the phone if I ever heard of a Volkswagen Golf. I said, "No, but I just can't believe you all are giving me a car. I just met you thirty minutes ago, and now you are telling me it's a Volkswagen!" I could sense that they were a little skeptical because it was a '93 and had a few beauty marks. They didn't know how I would respond, but I didn't care!

I knew this was God's doing. Of all of the cars in the world, it was not a coincidence. And it was free, which clearly means no payments! I have driven Orchid for the past two years, and I absolutely love her. She is a reflection of God's beauty and presence in my life and a constant reminder that good things—and sometimes even free things—come to those who wait.

I don't believe this would have happened if I had not made the decision on June 5, 2011 to pursue financial freedom and no longer be bound to an "I want it now" mentality. All I had in my beautiful designer purse was $0.74. While I was there, I did some shopping. In fact, the suit and accessories I wore that night were new. However, my wallet was empty, and so was my mentality (lacking substance).

As Bishop Lockett extended the opportunity for people to sow into their "Continual Increase Blessings", I walked up, bawling my eyes out. I excused myself from the sanctuary because I was crying so hard. I felt chains drop from me in that moment, and I knew that my life would never be the same. I held tight to that envelope because I was embarrassed and ashamed that all I had left was $0.74 to give because of the shopping spree that I had been on for the past few days.

God will use whatever you have left. It may not be much. Your heart may be torn into a million pieces, your account may be overdrawn, your life may be in shambles, or your spouse may have just walked out on you, but whatever you have left, God can use it and make something beautiful, creating a life-changing encounter forever. You don't have to stay stuck where you are. I didn't and will never be back in that place again.

Days after giving the last $0.74 that I had to my name, amazing blessings started to come. I was moving from Pittsburgh, Pennsylvania to British Columbia, Canada in about three weeks, and I knew that everything that God had blessed me with and continually blesses me with stems from the $0.74-seed that was sown in an atmosphere of continually increasing blessings. Sometimes we get caught up in what we have to give when God looks at our hearts in which we give.

There were two brothers in the Bible who gave sacrifices to God. Their names were Cain and Abel. Cain gave to God with limitation. He held back what was best for him, while Abel gave all to God, reserving nothing for himself. God was pleased with Abel because not only were his actions in line with God, but also his heart.

There is another account in the Bible that demonstrates the way God blesses us in return for what we give Him. In fact, you give your life to God, and He gives you a new one. You give your relationship to God, and He blows you away with someone who naturally has the ability to increase the quality of your life. I love that about God. I love how God takes what's small ($0.74) and decides to bless us with much just because He loves us.

God invites you to live a life that exceeds any and everything that you could ever imagine, and He delights in blessing you just because He loves you like that. Be still and willing to wait before making decisions, and remind yourself that there is beauty to be had, joy to be gained, and a life that is made available to you—the orchid life.

## CHAPTER 6

*I'm not one to take no for an answer. Behind every no, there is a yes waiting for you.*

I found my undergrad experience to be quite a journey. I went from rejection letter to acceptance letter. I went from no funds to practically receiving a full ride. I went from being told that the on-campus ministry that I had started was too loud to being asked to speak for chapel, which included the entire student body, faculty, and staff—what a journey indeed. However, the most interesting reoccurring journey that I experience in life is the process by which ministry opportunities are extended to me outside of the United States. It has been four years since I've lived in the United States, not including a seven-month waiting period. Ever since I was child, I knew that I was created to do something bigger than me and that the only reason God chose to use me was because I was willing.

When I think about what has happened in my life, the places that I've been able to travel to for God, and the people whom I've been privileged to meet, I am amazed and humbled. There are days when I just quietly sit still, thinking of everything that has taken place. We should never become so familiar with being blessed that we lose sight of the fact that we don't deserve it and that our blessings pale in comparison to anything that we could accomplish on our own.

Maybe I was born with a gift to speak comfortably before crowds. However, I don't believe that it is my natural ability or gift that people are drawn to me. I know for a fact that there is nothing great about Miracle Reed that would cause anyone to want to get to know me. But I recognize that God lives inside of me and draws people to me. I then lead them to Him. I am sure of that.

In being led by God, I had a sense that I was to place my resume online a few months before graduating from Geneva. I don't remember how I found ministry websites where positions were available for pastors, but I did. I had twenty-eight resumes placed around the world to various churches that were searching for pastors. During this time, I started to develop a Caribbean accent while I preached. It only became apparent while preaching or speaking before crowds, and then it went away.

I didn't understand it, and most of the time, I wasn't aware that it was happening. One day, a good friend of mine invited me to a hospital to pray for someone. I entered the room, and immediately, my American dialect was no more. For nearly two hours, I spoke with a Caribbean accent. The people looked at me quite strangely and insisted on knowing where I was originally from. They could not believe it, and after I realized what was happening, I was in shock as well.

After the prayer time was over and I left the hospital, I sat in my car and began to pray. I asked God what was going on and where these accents came from. God clearly said, "Miracle, these accents that you have picked up are representations of where I am sending you." I was confused, and at the time, I had no clue what God was referring to. The only place outside of the United States that I had traveled to was Mexico for a mission trip. I never pictured myself living anywhere outside of the United States until I started sending out my resumes.

At this point, I was going into my last semester at Geneva and had not received any positive feedback from the various places where I sent my resumes. However, I don't believe in taking no for an answer. If you are led to do something, there is a reason behind it, and you shouldn't stop until you find it. I continued to send out resumes, but after twenty-eight, I became a little discouraged and began to doubt. There is something to be said when discouragement comes even when you know with certainty what you are to do.

I was once again being set up for something that was bigger than me was part of God's plan. I will never forget the emotion and excitement that I felt when I read an e-mail from Senior Pastor Reginald Perry from St. Croix, Virgin Islands. The night before I received the response from Pastor Perry, I noticed a posting online for a church that was looking for a youth pastor. I had no idea where St. Croix was located, but I figured, "Hey, I've already placed twenty-eight; one more won't hurt." To my surprise, the next day, there was an e-mail waiting. I ran around Ms. Cook's house. I was uncontrollably excited; words do not capture what I felt.

I called my grandma, and she couldn't understand a word that I said. She encouraged me to calm down before I called this pastor in the Caribbean. So I did. Two months later, my grandma and I were flown to St. Croix. For the next five days, I was interviewed, ministered to the youth group, and met with various people. When most people think of the Caribbean, they immediately think of beach life or resort. This is part of the Caribbean, but there is much more. However, once I attended the Sunday morning service, I knew immediately that this would be the first place I would call home for ministry after graduating.

Victorious Believers Ministries gave me a great foundation and blessed me with a privileged opportunity. I didn't know why I was so eager to finish two degrees in a 3.5-year timeframe, but once this door opened, everything made sense. I move to the Virgin Islands ten days after I graduated from Geneva. It took twenty-nine resumes to get there, but when you believe that there is a yes behind the no, you will stop at nothing.

My life was forever changed as a result of accepting God's invitation to live a life without limits. I would have never imagined that the Virgin Islands would be a part of the plan, but God did. My eyes were opened to a life that exceeds what I thought. I tried to live in Maryland, and God was preparing to bless me with the Virgin Islands.

In this life, we can make plans that will more than likely become vetoed by God, or we can live life without plans and be blown away by every season we find ourselves in. I have not figured it all out, but I have learned how to live a life without plans. As a result, I am overwhelmed daily by the life that belongs to me just because I said, "Yes." Give God room to surprise you with resume number twenty-nine. He sure did it for me!

# CHAPTER 7

# *Plans Change*

*In this life, most of what is planned will change, whether it's the time, person, day, or season. The key in understanding change is welcoming it.*

Life is full of unexpected events—car problems, sick children, breakups, relocation, or natural catastrophic events in the world. One thing that is certain is change. As a matter of fact, the only constant we have in this life is change. We can try to avoid it, act like it doesn't exist, or even try to stop it from happening, but it is inevitable. We can add Botox, dye our hair, lose weight, or even change careers, but the truth remains; change is here to stay.

In this chapter, you will receive some valuable and helpful tools in dealing with the plans that have been vetoed in your life. You will learn how to properly respond to the invitation that is extended to you.

It is imperative to let go of self. This is one of the most challenging things you will have to do, and it will be a part of your process for as long as you live. It is not only an ongoing process, but also a process that will change depending on the season of life that you may find yourself in. The good thing is that you have time, and the more you incorporate the provided tools and tips into your life, the easier it will become to adapt to change. It will take some getting used to, and I do not claim to have made it. I am constantly in my own process of being open and available to whatever God wants to do, however He sees fit to do so.

This book is a great example. Less than a week ago, God spoke to me and said that I was getting ready to write another book. This is the second book that I've written; however, this will be the first one to be released. I was not overwhelmed by the idea of writing another book, but I was overwhelmed by the fact that I would start and finish in ten days because shortly following, I would begin the writing of another. That was overwhelming. As you read this chapter, take note of the fact that this is day two. I have eight more days to go, and the titles and ideas come as I sit in silence and concentrate.

I am the guest speaker at a Bible camp called Ness Lake. I wish you could see the living room-style bedroom that I am privileged to stay in for the next six days. The bedroom is furnished with two beds (with quilted bedding), a fireplace (not needed), a small round wooden table and four chairs, a leather couch, a full sink and mirror, three windows (with plaid curtains), and a balcony. I honestly can't think of a better place to write. I am in the middle of the woods, surrounded by a beautiful lake and the laughter of children outside my window. Truly, I have been blessed. However, this was not the room that was initially reserved for me—but plans changed!

As we take a look at various areas in which one might experience change, keep in mind the possibility of renewal, restoration, and forgiveness. In your process of welcoming change as a part of your plans being vetoed by God, keep in mind that this is indeed a process. Give yourself time, and don't give up on yourself, because this is a new way of thinking that will require you to let go of the old way. In life, change can either become your worst enemy or your best friend. The choice is placed in your hands. Are you ready for this? You are ready to unlock some doors in your life that have been closed for a very long time. Are you ready for the keys?

## Seven Keys to Welcoming Change

1. Understand that change is a part of life. In many ways, you have tried to understand change. The goal of change is not your complete understanding but your complete surrender. In other words, just let it happen. Do not spend another day trying to hold on to that which is changing right before your eyes, whether it's the car you can no longer afford, the friend who is no longer the same, or the wardrobe that no longer fits.
2. Understand that change is not always a bad thing. Most of the time, change is good because it allows you to see either areas of growth or areas where growth needs to take place. No matter how you look at it, change highlights areas of our lives that we may overlook.
3. Open your eyes to the blessings that come with change. Because we become content with what we know, we become quite uncomfortable with the idea of having to change. There are blessings that await your season of change. Welcome them!
4. Consider how refusing to accept change can keep you stuck and limited to plans that God has already vetoed. This is not the life that you want. You have a feeling deep down inside that there is more, and I encourage you to trust that. Refusing to accept change would be accepting a life of limits and constraints.
5. Acknowledge that having the ability to change is the best option you have in a world that looks for people who are naturally able to adapt. Your decision to welcome change is also your decision to welcome countless opportunities. When people have found someone who can adapt to change and be completely fine with it, they have found a gem. Allow your ability to change to become one of your greatest assets.
6. Look for opportunities to change. These can be changes in your habits, style, posture, vocabulary, way of life, route that you take home, etc. Change can become your best friend if

you let it. Change welcomes opportunity to become more skilled at your craft, whether that is being a husband, lawyer, wife, or teacher. Don't be afraid to take inventory of yourself.
7. Lastly, give people whom you trust a space in your life to share areas where they noticed you've become rigid. This will help you break away from the cycle of limitations and welcome a life of no limits. This is one of the most challenging keys, but we all need people like this in our lives.

These seven keys are only as effective as you allow them to be. If you give them room to show you a few things about yourself, they will become part of your way of thinking. I take time to evaluate areas that are not effective and areas where I could improve. At first, this was a challenge and quite burdensome, but as I began to make this a way of life, it became like second nature. I am highly organized by nature, and I create Word documents and lists for almost everything.

This tells you that I do not like to lose things. I enjoy order, and most of the time, I place everything in my house exactly where it was originally. Sometimes my family thinks I'm a bit extreme, and at times when I feel like I am becoming obsessive, I will purposely leave a few things out of place just so that I can reel myself back in concerning change. You may be laughing at me by this point. It's okay; my family does the same.

Those who know me get a big kick out of it, especially when they bring up the topic of children and marriage. People have said quite often to me, "Miracle, I can't wait for God to send you a husband and you start having children because it will totally mess up your organized life, and you will grow to love it!"

My response is always, "Yeah, I don't know about that." Life is fun, though. Who knows what God has in store? I don't have any plans. It is my hope and continual desire to be content in every season that I find myself in.

There was a man in the Bible by the name of Paul. He viewed life in the same way concerning contentment. He was never moved by what he had or did not have. He learned that the essence of life is to be content in all things. I agree completely. I would like to encourage you as well. The moment you become content with who you are and what you have will be the moment you really begin to live.

I am currently in a season of experiencing life for all that it has to offer. I am constantly trying new things, creating new projects, placing candid moments on Instagram, and looking for ways to inspire people around me. Too often, we waste our time worrying and doubting everything that we go through instead of accepting the fact that it happened, it hurt, and nothing will change it or give that time back. I became prey to that sort of thinking until I accepted that my plan was vetoed by God and that it could only mean that there is something better. This is a part of life; this is a part of change. Welcome it.

The list that I have made available to you is one that I use for myself as well. There were areas of my life that I had to give over to God, and it was not smooth sailing the entire time. There are lessons that I had to learn the hard way, just like you, but I am honestly thankful for every one of them. When you realize that no matter how you learned the lesson, the important thing is that you learned it, you begin to put away the negative stuff that surrounded the circumstance. This is a defining factor in growth, change, and your plans being vetoed by God.

The best thing about accepting the offer to live a life without limits is that you have no idea what's next, where you will be, or what you will end up doing. I never thought that I would live in Canada, but here I am—the little preacher girl, Miracle, from Wilkinsburg. Often, those who are used by God are those who are overlooked by people. I love to hear stories about people who were said to be hopeless and are on television discussing their Fortune 500 companies. You never know what will need to be vetoed in order to establish greatness. You must be willing to welcome the fact that more than likely, your plans will change!

# CHAPTER 8

## The Give-Up and the Gain

*In life, there will be much to give up. Keep your head up because there will also be much to gain.*

In a life of no limits, there will be much to give up. However, there will also be much to gain. One might spend his or her entire life trying to hold on to as much as he or she can only to find out that much of what he or she tried to keep will in some way be lost. In the Bible there were people who tried to hold on to life but ultimately lost it. There is something to be gained in the midst of that which is given up. As you learn to live a life that goes against everything you once thought to be true, you will need to just give it up. There will be a time to just let go of your life and welcome all that is to be gained from God.

God can do more for you than you can do for yourself. In fact, God is able to satisfy you with life to a degree that you've never imagined. The decision that goes along with receiving that life is contingent upon your willingness to give up that which you've held on to. You have the decision to either work most of your life or allow life to work for you. Your willingness to let go of yourself and welcome Him can make a difference in your career, family, relationships, finances, health, and pretty much every aspect of your life.

## WHEN GOD VETOES YOUR PLAN

People spend their entire lives trying to work as much as they can in order to have a substantial retirement fund. However, in this life of no limits, things work a lot differently. The principle of trying to do all that one can to ensure some level of security comes from a life that has been lived in limitation. This life is very similar to the spree mentality that was discussed in chapter 5, which is a mentality that responds in a way that demonstrates foreseen lack. This way of thinking is not welcomed in the invitation that is extended. In life, there are plenty of opportunities and much to gain. In the words of a good sister friend, "My father is not dead; I have access to all that I need."

When God vetoes your plan, He does so to prevent you from living your entire life in a cycle of limitation. What is extended to you is a life in which you will never have to wait for the deal, job, opportunity, or relationship of a lifetime because every single moment that you experience in life will exceed all that you've known before. You don't have to sit around, hoping and wishing that you finally get that promotion or meet the right person, because living this way will properly position you for everything that you have coming. You won't have to chase it; it will follow you along your path. As you grow to trust yourself and the abilities that you have, you will then learn to lean on God for direction. This is the beginning of understanding the process of the give-up and the gain.

I used to think that God wanted me to give up everything for Him. Now I know for a fact He does. I wrote a blog in 2012 that was titled "I'm dying." People read the blog and sent me messages that read, "Miracle, are you okay? You aren't really dying, are you?" I found it to be quite interesting because my writing concerning a surrendered life to a plan that is bigger than me made others feel uncomfortable. I even had a friend say to me, "This is the last blog that I will read from you. This has been way too earth-shatteringly relevant." Even in her reading of it, something began to happen on the inside that this person could not ignore. God was calling for her to come and live a deeper life that is not crafted by human ideas but led by the presence of God.

I used to think that everything was not for everyone, but I no longer believe that. Everyone is meant to live life without limits, but people choose what they want. It's not a matter of it not being for everyone; it's a matter of being willing to make it your life. I wrote that blog at a time in my life when I tried to make a few things happen and did some serious snacking. I knew that there would come a time where God would once again put my life in balance with His will, and that was the time. He made it clear that I had two options; I could either waste time by postponing that which was inevitable, or I could be honest with myself. I chose the latter.

Not only did I choose the latter, but I also wanted to be used as an example for people to see that this life will require Miracle to die. I realized that I could not make another decision based on personal gain. I can't accept God and keep me. I needed to go—and not just some of me, but all. At that moment on October 13, 2012, I died to my dreams, plans, and ways and welcomed a life with no plan or limits that consistently leaves me intoxicated by the beauty of all that has been made available.

The truth is that we all have the ability to give up everything for God, but the fact is that many of us will choose not to. Many of you will read this book and genuinely desire to welcome the fact that plans change, but something will get in the way of your willingness. That something is you. You see, there is no way that you can gain without giving up something. That something may be your time, a drink, or the magazines that you keep stowed away. Only you know what that something is, and only you can make the decision to give it up in order to gain.

I recall a time in high school when I was asked to minister at a weekend church retreat. I accepted the invite and was excited until something else came up. To my surprise and dismay, my school planned the annual Snowball dance the same weekend. I was torn because I really wanted to attend the school dance; yet I have never been one to go back on my word.

Although I wrestled with calling the church and telling them that I could not make it, I knew in my heart even back then that my yes to God would at times get in the way of my plans. It didn't take long for me to welcome the proper perspective concerning the situation, and before I knew it I was no longer concerned about the school dance. About a week before both the church retreat and the school dance, I received a phone call informing me that the retreat needed to be canceled due to unforeseen events.

Was this God's doing? I believe so. I believe that in living life without limits, there will be tests that come along the way to challenge us and reveal what's in our hearts. I made the decision to not only keep my word, but also to see the privilege in serving God and loving people. As a result of my ability to adapt to change, God not only honored that, but also allotted me the opportunity to attend the dance.

God wants to know that He is number one and that nothing and no one is capable of having a reserved spot in your life when you live life without plans. There will be much to give up in this life, but there is no comparison to all that will be gained.

# CHAPTER 9

## Bounce Back

*The defining factor of being prepared for relationships—whether romantic or friendship — is the ability to bounce back. This is resilience.*

In my teen years, I lived a very focused life—even more so than I do now. I not only attended school during the day, but was also enrolled in Bible school at night, led Generation for Christ on the weekends, and traveled almost every weekend to minster on Sunday mornings. Did I mention that I was cheerleader during this period as well? As I look back over my life, I often wonder when I slept and how I had the time to do both, but somehow, I did. There are no limits in God, only that which we create.

However, in being extremely busy with life, I struggled with knowing how to balance friendships. Often, I didn't know if I was looked at as a friend or counselor. At times, it was quite confusing and challenging to handle. As a child, I had a very close friend. We planned to do everything together—be in each other's weddings, go on trips, you name it. However, plans change, and often people do as well. I had to learn very quickly what it would mean for me to be able to bounce back when what I thought was secure would in many ways no longer exist.

I found myself as a teenager trying to capture friendships like that of my childhood, but it never quite worked. I now know as an adult that it was not meant to. Those experiences in life were meant to create an innate ability to bounce back. Now that I travel and am relocated every few years, I've learned how to manage friendships a lot better than before. I could still use some smoothing out, but overall, I've become quite resilient.

My high school years were full of dances, basketball games (cheerleading), preaching, and traveling. My life was indeed full, but my friendships seemed to lack the consistency that I desired. Now, don't get me wrong. I've been surrounded by crowds of people my entire life and have many guys who I call my bros and girlfriends who are sisters to me. However, during high school, it was challenging as a preacher. There's an underlying feeling that makes you feel like you just don't quite fit in. I wasn't created to fit but to stand out.

God began to bless me with some amazing women who I am still friends with to this day. God used them to help reestablish my views on what a friendship looked like. They gave me the opportunity and freedom to just be me, and though our friendships have not been perfect, they have certainly been transparent. God used these friendships to create in me the ability to bounce back and welcome people in my life, though there are no guarantees. I have a great gift in them.

In life, we form ideas based on what we've experienced, whether good or bad. Show me someone who has been in horrible relationships, and I will show you someone who struggles with trust issues. This is life, and how we process what we've gone through in life will shape our perspectives. The unfortunate thing about negative experiences is that we tend to build walls. We are often unaware that this is what we do. Have you ever recalled a response that you gave someone concerning another person and later realized that your response came out as if you had not forgiven that person—like you were bitter or like it happened just yesterday? I'm sure we can all say "Yes" to some degree. This happens because we have not dealt with the situation properly and continue to carry it in our hearts.

You are only as free as you allow yourself to be. Though you may appear free before others, you know good and well that you have tried to ignore that which you now classify as being nonexistent. You know the responses we give when we try to downplay situations that really bother us. "Who? Oh, him." "Man, please—she wasn't all that. She had a stuck-up attitude anyway." "I wasn't really interested in that job." "He didn't make enough money anyway." "I was tired of dealing with that landlord; I was planning on moving out a while ago." All of these responses seemingly display disconnect from the situation. However, it is apparent that no matter how we try to skirt around issues, they will not go away, as they are boxed and sealed. You must give yourself the needed time to bounce back from disappointment because only then will you truly become free.

People have a way of stripping you of your personal worth and value. We give them that influence and involvement in our lives. Even a child knows what's his or hers. A child will tell you in a heartbeat, "Mine." How is it that a child enters into this world with an innate ability to define what rightfully belongs to him or her, but as adults, we find ourselves giving what rightfully belongs to us away to undeserving people? Maybe you can help me out with this one because I have yet to come up with a response. I have a series of possibilities that include obligation, guilt, compassion, genuine need, and concern. However, none of these lead me to understand how we can so easily lose sight of who we are and what we were created to do.

Have you ever been around a person who always shares with you how much fun they had back when? You get to the point where you think, *Okay, okay already; new memories, please and thank you.* Most people aren't content with who they are today, and they have to live in what was or what they think will be. Interestingly enough, I have found this to be true everywhere I've lived.

People don't know how to respond when I say, "I am completely in love with where I live." They all give me a look that says, *You've got to be kidding me.* I guess I understand their response because if I had not accepted the invitation to live life without limits, I am certain my response would be a lot different. I have come to the conclusion that when you go with the flow, your life begins to follow a rhythm that only you can understand.

I spent a lot of my earlier days in life, ministry, and the dating world worrying about what's next. Then I realized that it didn't matter what was next. It doesn't even matter what was; all that matters is what's now. Once I gained that key, I began to unlock many doors in my life and experience the ability to bounce back from every decision and mistake that I've made.

Don't allow what was or what you think will be to make you lose sight of what you have right now. I robbed myself of the beauty of various seasons that I found myself in because I lacked the ability to bounce back, but once I grabbed hold of this key called resilience, there was no stopping me. I invite you to welcome the gift of becoming resilient. I am not saying that you have to ignore what has happened in your life. But you will never be healed staying there. In other words, deal with how you feel, be honest with yourself, confess if you feel it's needed, and move on. It can be very dangerous to not allow yourself to move on.

This is the main reason most people live in self-condemnation. Some even hate themselves because they can't get over what was done to them or what they've done to another. This is your chance to be free from that, from yourself, and from everything that comes along with lacking the ability to move on. Don't spend another day stuck.

### Declare these words over your life:

> I am not defined by what I've done. I am not defined by what has been done to me. My life is not limited to my experiences or to what I have convinced myself of. I have the ability and choice to welcome freedom in my life, and in this moment, I say "Yes" to freedom. I realize that this is an ongoing process and that there will be people, situations that get in the way of my decision to welcome freedom. But God, I ask you to veto my plan, my thoughts, and any habit that would keep me from the

life that I have been invited to live. More than anything, I desire to live a life that leaves me intoxicated by the beauty of every season that I find myself in. Hello, new season; I welcome you. Intoxicate me.

You may think, *Miracle, is it really as easy as declaring some words, and ta-da?* Well, yes and no. Living a life without limit is as easy as declaring words, but it's not so easy to fully believe them. Because both speech and belief are needed, unfortunately it's not as easy as only declaring words, but that is half of it. How do you get to a place where you actually believe what you say? How do you change the way you think when you have been told your entire life to forgive but never forget? The answer is not overly complicated. You just stop. You may ask, "What do you mean, you just stop?" You just stop believing the lies and stop believing that you are incapable of becoming a different person.

For the majority of my life, my parents were drug-addicted. As a result of that, I spent a good portion of my life burdened and worried about pretty much everything, though I was extremely busy and focused. There were days when I didn't know if I would see my mom again. There were nights when I feared the results of my mom's decisions. There were years that passed before I would see my dad, and unfortunately, there were days when I hated my life. All the while, I preached and became well-known in my city. I was awarded with multiple honors and received multiple opportunities to share the love of Christ with people. But I was confused and uncertain about who I was. I struggled with understanding how and why God would use me with a family like mine. My grandmother was life to me. Of course, she takes no credit for the way that I turned out, but honestly, I don't know where I would be without her.

During my earlier years of life, my mom was unable to take care of me, though she lived in the house with my grandma and two uncles. Her addiction was her love, and unfortunately, as any child, I didn't understand. But my grandma made it clear to me that my mom experienced a sickness and addiction that took over her life. She told me that she didn't want to be that way but that the addiction had control over her. I prayed, cried, and did not understand why things would not change.

It seemed like the more I prayed, the worse things became. But God told me one day, "Miracle, just stop. You can't change her; only I can." From that day forward, a burden was lifted. God gave me the ability in that moment to bounce back from the hurt, neglect, and every negative thought that I had experienced in my life. In this moment, God is saying the same to you. Bounce back, get yourself together, and realize that despite all that has taken place in your life, you are still here, and there is work for you to do.

Many years later, my dad came to see me. I can't remember how many years it was since I saw him, but I remember waiting at the Greyhound bus station in downtown Pittsburgh for him to come. My mom didn't have enough heart to tell me that once again, he would not be there. I cried my eyes out and did not understand why he didn't want to see me. I didn't know at the time that his addiction was also the love of his life. After many years of great challenges and triumph, there are days when I can't believe my eyes.

My parents were separated for seventeen years. My mom lived in Pittsburgh, and Dad lived in Buffalo, New York, where I was born. In a way that only He could, God decided to place them back in each other's lives. It's been some years since the bounce-back took place, and each day, the journey continues. I don't profess to have figured out what God is doing—and to be honest, I have no interest in figuring it out. For the first time, I have a healthy relationship with both my mom and dad; for that, I am grateful. You never know what God has planned, but you can trust that what He has for you is good. At times, it comes in unexpected ways.

There have been many times when I felt myself getting in God's way and trying to create nonexistent plans for my family. A mental billboard will appear that reads, "When God vetoes your plan, step back." Each day, I make a decision to step back. I make the decision to love my parents and honor them for who they are. There have even been times when I have called my dad in the wee hours of the morning to give him words that God gave me for him.

I will not act as if my process has been easy, because it certainly hasn't, but my process has brought me great triumph and has shaped me into the woman I am today. As a result of this process of freedom, forgiveness, and restoration, I have experienced and welcome the people God has placed in my life. I love those who are already there. This is the key to a life that is able to bounce back.

My dad is one of the funniest people I know when it comes to ways in which a person carries themselves. In many ways his personality is like the joy that children experience when they are excited about something new that they have received. My mom, on the other hand, is a bit more selective concerning the things that excite her. My grandma is Grandma, and she does what she wants! She is a rock and gives her strength to us all. If and when I become a grandma, I pray that I have her heart to love relentlessly. She has the ability to bounce back and love like there is no tomorrow.

If love had a face outside of Jesus, I am convinced that it would be that of my grandma. You would be amazed by all that she has been through, all that she has taken from others, and the way she stands above it all. I am convinced that God gave grandmas a special ability to bounce back.

Go to the thoughts section of this book, and write down five things that have hurt you the most. You may think that I say things in a simple way—and you are right. I do. At times, we make our life experiences so deep and overly complicated that we never get to the root of them. That's a bright red flag! Anything that tries to camouflage itself in your life by becoming so deep and complicated that it cannot be discussed is a clear trap to keep you from being healed.

It is my prayer that you are able to say, "It happened, I was confused, I did it, and it hurt, but now it's time for me to move on." Once again, this is a personal exercise for your growth and ability bounce back from what you've gone through. If you can't be honest with yourself, who can you be honest with? Let's get down to it!

1. Make a list of the five things that have hurt you the most.
2. Write your responses to those things when they occurred.

3. Explain the feelings that you experienced as a result of what took place.
4. Describe how you feel when you see people who were involved in what happened.
5. Jot down a few outcomes that would be ideal concerning what happened.

Look at what you've written, and declare that you no longer desire to be stuck in your response to number three. Those feelings are still very much alive. When you see those people, there is still a sting that remains. Now take another step. Write a letter of forgiveness (not to be mailed or discussed) to each person who was involved in your top five list. This is for your personal healing process. Declaring those words of forgiveness and writing to those who have hurt you will free you in a way you never imagined. This may be the most challenging thing that you have been asked to do.

You may say, "Miracle, I just can't do that." Can you not do it, or do you choose not to do it? If it is the latter, then that would also mean that you choose to stay stuck and wounded. This prevents you from being able to love and receive love freely. I know that this is a challenge. You may not have thought that I would ask something like this of you, but this is what happens when God vetoes your plan.

I can only extend to you what I have tried and know has worked in my life. Even as I write, I am thinking of a letter that I need to write and pray over. My stomach dropped as I began to write this section because I know exactly what God wants me to do as well. I will never give advice that I have not taken part in.

Life is interesting—the more you live and let go, the more you gain! I sit here at 1:44 a.m., thrilled by life, intoxicated by this season, and blown away by the grace of God. There is just something about being transparent before God. He doesn't always ask you to do the unthinkable (the most vulnerable act of forgiveness that one could display), but He does have you ponder it from time to time. It definitely gets your heart rate going.

Do you believe that you are able to live a free life this year? You are!

**There are three key elements that define who a person becomes and how he or she obtains a free life:**

1. *You are what you believe.* You are what you believe about yourself—what you believe you can have and deserve. Your understanding of God plays a major role in being what you believe as well. The amount of influence He has in your life and your willingness to accept Him into your life carry major weight in identifying what you believe.
2. *You are what you feed yourself.* This is not limited to what you allow in but includes what you allow others to feed you as well. Sometimes we have not made certain decisions or choices directly. However, we become impacted by the decisions that we allow other people to make around us.
3. *You are who you hang around.* There is no escaping the fact that you are a mirror reflection of the company that you keep. Naturally, my personality is quite introverted. People are pretty shocked when they learn this about me because of the confidence that God allows me to possess—not only as I write, but also as I stand before crowds of people and speak. Because I am my family's only child and grandchild, I have mastered self-entertainment in many ways. We can also be impacted and influenced by the people we don't allow in. There is a fine line between the two, and it is different for every person.

These three keys are instrumental in understanding your personal freedom, ability to bounce back, and ability to recognize your own strengths. Don't allow yourself to become limited because you stand in your own way. Step back, and welcome the art and skill of living a resilient life. This positions you in a good place to welcome others in and escort others out! Don't worry; they will eventually bounce back.

# CHAPTER 10

## Go with the Flow

*There is a rhythmic flow to life that does not move too fast or too slow. Finding the rhythm of your life creates that flow.*

I never imagined that I would teach a hip-hop class in the Caribbean, but I did. I wasn't aware that I had the ability to choreograph, let alone teach a group of teenager's routines, but I did. I sat at my desk and had a God-inspired moment. I was to start a gospel hip-hop dance team called DGT (doing great things). I then found a song by gospel hip-hop artist Canton Jones called "Doing Great Things!" I was in shock as to how everything came together. Before I knew it, I went to the gym to work on choreography, and within a few weeks, practice began.

It is amazing how God connects us with the right people at the right time. I was headed to church one evening, and a familiar face pulled up in a car beside me. He asked where I was going, and I told him, "Church." He then gave me a ride. Interestingly enough, we met at church a few weeks prior. As he dropped me off at church, I mentioned that I was getting ready to start a gospel hip-hop team. His response was very close to, "No way; are you serious?" Long story short, he became an instrumental leader, choreographer, and breakdancer of DGT as well as a leader at the church.

In life, there are no certainties concerning what will happen from day to day, but the mystery in living a life without limits makes the journey that much more exciting. I lived in the Caribbean, preaching, teaching, praying, counseling, and making up dance moves. Who would have thought? Not me. But God knew that there would be many lessons learned and taught along the journey.

I find myself receiving strange looks when certain questions are asked. For example, people ask quite often, "How and why did you come from living in the Virgin Islands to living not only in Canada, but northern Canada, at that?" Of course, there is a story behind what led me to Canada, but my response is, "I'm just going with the flow."

There is a clear and distinct rhythm that has followed me every day of my life. I have not always understood it, but I have always followed it. There are people who make themselves available for any and everything, no matter what it may require of them, and then there are people who live their lives limited to what they think is possible. My entire life, I have followed the former. I have been crazy enough to believe that one can accomplish anything that he or she is bold enough to pursue. This is how I believe life was meant to be lived.

The rhythm that I speak of has been, "Are you up for it?" Up to this point, my answer has always been, "Sure, why not?" I continue to live my life that way every day. However, I have not always been this way. Though there were clear signs that I was invited to live a life without limits, I wasn't quite ready to let go of my plans. I was determined, and in my mind, there was nothing wrong with the plans that I had. Does that sound familiar?

What I desired didn't seem like too much to ask. I wanted a master's degree, a husband, and to travel the world while I had the luxury of being extremely comfortable in my home in Maryland. Clearly, God vetoed those plans. Who's to say what will one day be? However, we do not live in what's next but in what's now, we must continue to be presently focused and driven. This is the rhythm that I live by—not too fast (not what's next) or too slow (what was), but just the right rhythm for my current life.

Once you find the rhythm of your life, you will then find the beat that creates the flow. You will know when you are off beat, because you will experience friction, frustration, and a lack of patience. You feel great peace and contentment in life when you find your flow. Your role is to go with the flow, not to create the flow. There is a specific flow that has already been a part of your life; you just have to take the time to seek it out. The time that is spent trying to create your own rhythm can be taken to get on beat. Don't get off beat by trying to create a rhythm that is too fast or too slow in comparison to what has already taken place.

My Orchid is a stick shift, and when I first saw the beloved clutch, my heart sank. I was extremely excited to have Orchid, but I was discouraged and thought that I would never learn how to drive her. I had one lesson in the car and was completely embarrassed because I stalled at every red light and stop sign. It's a good thing I live in Canada; no one honked the horn. In fact, people put their hands up like, *It's okay; we will wait for you*—which could also be interpreted as, *Poor child doesn't have a clue what she is doing, Bless her little heart.* Whatever they meant, I was appreciative for it rather than the sound of honking horns!

While I had the driving lesson, I was told to just *feel the car* and something about releasing the clutch. Of course, right—feel the car? I didn't even know it was possible to *feel the car* until I had another driving lesson in a large parking lot. Within two hours, I was ready to hit the road. With time and patience, I caught on to what *feeling the car* meant. It's been two years since I started the amazing journey of NASCAR! I'm just kidding—but people do I say I drive Orchid like a racecar.

Once I got the hang of driving, I began to enjoy it. I actually have become quite biased at this point. I find excitement in controlling the car; I feel like I'm much safer when I'm in control. The car flows to the beat that I create; we flow together. In order to obtain the rhythmic flow of your life, you may need a few lessons to help you. I did. It does not happen overnight, but it does happen as often as you allow it. Feel, learn, and go with the rhythmic flow of your life.

# CHAPTER 11

## Oh, Canada

*I never thought I would end up in Canada.
I am thankful that life is not about what I
think but about what God knows.*

If only life were as simple as a microwave. No effort would be needed for anything because everything is ready-made. Can you imagine? We would all live as robots—more so than we do now! This is the complete opposite of the life that you are invited to live. Life has twists and turns.

If you work by a clock, life is sometimes late. If you work by your account, life is sometimes bankrupt. But when you begin to live life without limits, your life is free from a waiting period, because every moment that you find yourself in is linked to a bigger picture. This is a concept that I wish everyone could adapt to. It is amazing to live each day. The ability to live without worrying about that which is temporary is something that most people never quite figure out. It took some time for me to fully grasp this concept as well.

I felt the tug of transition, which was challenging especially with the connections that were made. I had lived in the Virgin Islands for two years and felt God was leading me to something else. I had no idea what I would do next or where I was going, but I figured that because I always have a home in Pittsburgh, that's where I would go during the waiting period. Making the decision to leave the Virgin Islands was one of the hardest decisions that I've made, but I knew that I had finished God's assignment.

Upon leaving the Virgin Islands, I received three calls from churches in the United States that were interested in having me be part of their pastoral staff. One I knew was not for me, the second generated great excitement, and the third I knew was led by God. Little did I know what would take place yet again.

The third call was Executive Pastor Laurey Berteig from a church in the state of Washington, close to the Seattle area. Though I have never been to Seattle, I've always had a fascination with it. I love rain. The phone interview was mind-blowing, for this church and the man interviewing me seemed completely taken. He mentioned that he had a stack of over 100 resumes on his desk for the position, but God would not let him put my down.

Pastor Bertieg felt that he had to speak with me. He offered a word of prayer with me. You may think this would be common in this sort of setting, but it's not. In fact, as he prayed for me, I became overwhelmed with emotion due to his sincerity and began to cry. After the prayer, the conversation was over, and he said that he would get back to me. Time passed, and I eventually heard from him. He informed me that the church was considering someone else for the position but that he would like to keep in contact with me, if I was okay with it. By this point, I couldn't tell you how many people have said that they would like to keep in contact with me for ministry-related reasons. I didn't think I would ever hear from him again.

Three long months passed since the transition back from the Virgin Islands. I was restless, frustrated, and a bit discouraged. Though my family and friends were glad to have me back home, I was not exactly thrilled to be there. After living in the Caribbean, I was extended the opportunity to see other places, and to go back home seemed like a step back in my mind. I had resumes all over the place for all sorts of jobs. All I knew was that I did not want to live in Pittsburgh. I guess many people are like that—we see a few places, and all of a sudden, we forget where we came from! I thank God for putting me in check about that!

My grandma offered to help me pay for grad school. However, I wasn't motivated to go. I value education but felt like my path began to take a different route. I felt that someone needed me, and I couldn't be available to others while sitting in a classroom at this point. Three months after my move to Pittsburgh, I received an e-mail from the pastor in Washington. What I read would change the course of my life once again. He informed that he had a brother who was also a pastor and lived in Canada. He was currently looking for an associate pastor who could work with youth and young adults, and the pastor told his brother all about me. I read this e-mail and instantly began to run around the house.

I began to communicate with Pastor Paul Berteig, who is the brother of Pastor Laurey Berteig (Washington). After a series of God-winks (occurrences that can only be attributed to God) I was asked to be interviewed via Skype. A woman at the interview also received a word for me. As I listened to this woman that I'd never met, I was floored. The specific details that God had revealed to her about me were mind-blowing. As the interview continued, I felt that God was present. Once the interview was over, the pastor said that he would contact me in a few days.

A few days turned into a few hours, and before the day was over, plans were made to fly me to Canada to be interviewed in person. Time is no factor with God. Three weeks later, I was flown to British Columbia, Canada. It was the most exhausting flight that I had ever been on, and words do not properly convey how tired I was after fourteen hours.

I landed in the city of Prince George, and the first thing that I noticed was an unusual and unpleasant smell. I asked what the smell was, and one of the leaders responded, "That's the smell of money"—pulp mills. I was completely exhausted from traveling, but to my surprise, one of the women from the church was excited to welcome me and had planned to take me to a dance competition. As soon as those lights went off in the auditorium, my eyes were closed for the rest of the production. The invitation was a kind gesture, but this little lady was beat.

As the days went on, I met with a series of leaders. I was invited to various dinners, and to my surprise, everyone who I met seemed to be extremely down-to-earth and authentic. However, there was one question that was answered that I could not quite make out. During the interview process, I asked what the diversity level was on a scale of one to ten. The pastor informed me that it was about seven. To my surprise, I hadn't seen a single a person of color. I was definitely the minority at Geneva, but when I was told the diversity level was seven, I assumed I would see some evidence of that. Little did I know that God was removing every limit in my life concerning cultural relativity.

Sunday rolled around, and I got ready for the service. I would minister in the morning as well as in an evening service for women. However, that morning, something interesting took place. I had a strange pain my eye, which never happens. I couldn't figure it out, and then God revealed to me that there would be someone in the service who had problems with his or her eye. I was to pray for that person. I go with the flow, so I thought, *No problem, God; whatever you say. I'm in.*

I arrived at the playhouse, which is the location of the services. I looked around discreetly, still trying to figure out how the pastor came up with the level of diversity. The interesting thing about life is that many times, we don't realize that we live in a box until we are forced to come out of it. God was inviting me to a life that would never see cultural relativity as grounds for any decision in life again. I didn't realize that I was searching for what I was comfortable in when God was beckoning me to come to the deep end of life and not remain in the shallow end. Never allow your "Yes" to be dictated by your level of comfort. Most of what we find comfort in is what will keep us stuck in lives of limits.

The presence of God was strong during the service, and by the end, practically the whole church came to the front to receive prayer. I was blown away by God's presence and the response of the people.

They were hungry for more of God and willing to wait for at least an hour for me to pray for them. It seemed to me that as soon as I opened my eyes after ending a prayer, more people appeared. It was amazing. It was humbling. It was God.

The following day, I transitioned to another host family who invited the whole church to come over and fellowship with me. This family has been blessed. As I arrived at the house, I was greeted by many people with warm smiles and hugs. I have never met such a warm and genuinely hospitable group in all my life. I didn't know what to think of it. Throughout the evening, I noticed various accents. The pastor was right; diversity certainly permeated the community. There were people at the house from various countries. It was amazing.

That night, I called my grandma and shared with her all that took place. I had never experienced so much love in a room at one time. I was treated kindly over the years in my travels, but there was something different about the way the people welcomed me in. It was a tangible display of generosity and kindness—something that was completely real. I was overwhelmed with thinking that this must be what heaven looks like—people from various countries, nations, and tongues.

I went to sleep that night in awe of what took place—not only at the church, but also at this lovely home. A day or two later, I flew back to Pittsburgh. Once I arrived, I had some praying to do. I knew that in order for me to make a transition like this, I would need God to open my eyes to see life, ministry, and church in a different way. I was invited to live a life that would confront every judgment and critical thought that had ever entered my mind. I was invited to live a life with no limits.

I was raised in a black nondenominational church that was very charismatic and Spirit-led. The music was vibrant, and there was a collective sense that everyone came to do the same thing—praise God for a few hours. Timbers Community Church is much different from anything that I have ever been a part of. It's beginning to sound like God was ready to veto my plan and my place of comfort, doesn't it?

## WHEN GOD VETOES YOUR PLAN

Timbers is a Christian Missionary and Alliance church. There is a strong emphasis on missions with Pentecostal roots. Services are held in a theater, the attire is "come as you are," and worship resembles Hill Song rather than Kirk Franklin or William McDowell. God was getting ready to take my preconceptions about church, people, and music; stomp on them; and then ask, "Is this what you were looking for?" Don't be alarmed; some areas of my life need to be broken down that way, or I won't understand them.

The next few weeks consisted of me preaching at various churches in my city and praying about whether Canada was the next assignment that God wanted me to accept. I sat in a church service, prepared to take the mic and preach, but something happened just as I was introduced. I took out a piece of paper and wrote down the words, "The door has been opened; walk through it." Tears began to flow instantly. I was in an area called Canonsburg.

I began to write down more words. "Your words will be likening unto a canon. They will come forth with great power. I am placing you in pastures. This will be a time of refreshing—a cool season, for you have made it through the heat." You may think that there is no way I received all that within a few minutes, but I did. I shared with the church that night what had happened just minutes before taking the podium. My heart raced the entire time, and I knew Canada was next. This would be a journey that would open my eyes and expose me to a life and love that would completely blow me away.

I went through a process of accreditation in the United States in order to make the transition to Canada for Timbers Community Church. I did not know the life that waited for me. From the moment I stepped off the plane, I was greeted by tons of people with flowers and hugs. I was blessed to have a fully furnished home with décor that was based on personal interest. I received Orchid one month later and was blessed with my Canadian family who shared the same last name (Johnson) as my grandmother. I was extended the opportunity to be the first woman and first person of color to be a keynote speaker during a leadership retreat. I had one of the most loving, transparent, down-to-earth, authentic, and passionate senior pastors (Paul Berteig) that I've ever known. I was privileged to be a part of an amazing ministry that stands on being a "come as you are," "church for the rest of us" place.

I knew that I was in the right place. I used to say that life couldn't get any better, but each day, it does. God makes sure of it. I am convinced that when God really wants to pour out His love, He sends people to do it.

Timbers Community Church is unlike any other ministry that I have been part of or seen. It thrives off of building community, life groups, and keeping constant communication as a family unit. We have two morning services on Sundays that are very intentional in being sensitive to where each person is in his or her understanding of God. As a result of that, we get many people through the doors who have never stepped foot in church or heard of Daniel, Joseph, or Paul. We love it that way and make it known that at Timbers that one needs no previous church experience. I love it.

The community that I am a part of has taught me more about myself than I could have ever imagined. I was welcomed to a life where there are no limits. It's amazing. I have no clue what's next, and I absolutely love living that way. It takes the pressure off of trying to figure things out.

In this life, we are extended the opportunity to accept many offers. However, most of the offers that we take up require a lot from us, and the return is often minimal (if any at all). I would like to think that there are opportunities that are created and tailored to our specific needs, but if we take up every offer that comes our way, we will never be available for that which was created for us. This works with snacks as well as overall life decisions. There is a specific job, person, and timeframe when you will have your first child. Don't rush it.

The fact that I am in Canada has nothing to do with me but all to do with God. I never applied for a job in Canada, but God knew that this is where I would be, despite me getting in the way of the process. God knew why He connected me to the pastor in Washington. He knew that behind the "No," there would soon be a "Yes" to follow. Do not become discouraged by the "No" answers that come your way, because soon a "Yes" will follow.

# CHAPTER 12

# *The Lie of Limit in the Midst of Abundance*

*There are no limits in life—only those that you create.*

Have you ever felt like the more steps you take forward, the more you take back? You may wonder how in the world you could make such progress and yet have so many setbacks. People have wondered this for many years, only to find an answer that will more than likely be overlooked. The reason we make progress in multiple areas of our lives and become set back in the same moment is due to a mind-set that is stuck in a cycle—it's cyclical thinking. Cyclical thinking keeps us spinning our wheels, never really believing that we deserve to reach that goal, no matter how attainable it may be.

Cyclical thinking could also be classified as self-sabotage—inner doubt that causes you to ruin the success of any and everything that you try to go after simply because you don't believe enough in yourself, therefore motivating you to quit at some point. How does one get stuck in a cycle like that? The reasons vary from person to person; however, the way by which one gets out of the cycle does not. It is the same for everyone. You must recognize that you have believed the lie of limit. This lie continually reminds you that you aren't good enough, educated enough, or have enough money to deserve to live a life of freedom. This lie will keep you limited and never fulfilling the purpose for which you were created.

**The lie of limit will tell you three main things:**

1. God is trying to keep things from you.
2. You are too limited in your resources to have what is needed.
3. You are damaged goods, undeserving of anything abundant.

These three lies are seeds that are sown into the lives of many people. This happens due to various circumstances, such as family situations, shame, poverty, abuse, neglect, unmet needs, or bad experiences concerning religion. However, just because you may identify with some of these instances, this does not mean that you are destined to live a life of limit. In fact, every time God vetoes your plan, He tries to open your eyes to see the ways in which limits have become a way of life for you. He certainly does not try to keep anything from you; He actually wants to do just the opposite.

God wants to expose you to a life of abundance. I am an example of God bringing a person out of a mindset of limit and exposing her to a life of abundance. He has made an example out of my life, and He wants to do the same for you. Only you are able to identify how those lies have taken root in your life, and only you can make the decision to put a stop to it. Make it your priority to take inventory of all that is in your heart that keeps you from maintaining steady progress. You don't have to see setbacks every few days when you are created for success in every aspect of the word.

Self-sabotage and cyclical thinking will keep your life on repeat. You will begin to think, *Didn't this just happen? Was I not just there? Did I not just say that?* The answer is yes, you have and you did, and you will continue to do so until you let go of your plan and stop trying to figure out that which no longer exists. Have you ever seen or read about people who become bankrupt within a few years of becoming millionaires? The world sits and wonders how that could happen. How someone could have so much and lose it so quickly is a mystery to most. But those people had the spree mentality.

The mentality that creates behavior and a way of life that robs a person of everything he or she has is the lie of limit in the midst of abundance. The lie that is believed comes out of a state of mind that becomes a person's way of life. The lie is that no matter what you have, you must remain in a state of poverty because of what you've been told and what you've allowed others to feed you. This lie of deception creeps up in subtle ways and distorts truth, causing one to believe that he or she must spend now because he or she may lose it later, be asked for it by family and friends, or not have a chance to enjoy it.

However, there is good news. Life was not meant to be lived as if it would run out. It was meant to be lived freely, being spent on that which will produce something that is far greater than what the eye can see—abundance. The life that we are invited to live is that of abundance, not of lack. I say this not only in a literal sense, but also in terms of a state of mind. Keep in mind that wealth is not a state of being but more a state of mind. This is the honest truth that the world does not want you to know.

The counselor won't tell you that you lost everything because in your mind, you never had it. But the truth remains that in your mind, you had nothing. It didn't matter what was given or received; in your mind, you remained limited. This is not the invitation that is extended to you. All of your plans that are vetoed by God will not be used against you. In fact, they will be used to show you your greatness and the fact that you actually deserve a better life.

You are invited to live a life where limits do not exist. There will be no limit to what you can do that you are willing to pursue. There will be no limit to what you can have, because the entire world has been created for you. This life is made available to you. Will you accept the offer or stay in cyclical thinking, remaining stuck in the lie of limit, while you are in the midst of abundance?

# CHAPTER 13

# Walks in the Park

*I used to think I needed someone to join me at the park. Now I know that someone is there already waiting for my arrival.*

Have you ever felt like you needed someone with you in order to accomplish something, whether great or small? I spent many years fighting the fact that I was on a path alone. I didn't quite understand why it always seemed as if I was asked to do something that no one else could do or was interested in doing. Eventually, I realized that life is much like the path that has always been before me. It's quiet and peaceful, and very seldom do I see anyone in front of or behind me. All that is there is what I create or allow to be created. However, there are undertones of passion, excitement, mystery, and enchantment.

There are moments in life when you know that all that you have is all you need, and then there are moments when you let go of what you have only to find that it was all that you needed. You needed nothing more, and you needed nothing less. However, when one takes his or her eyes off of what he or she has, that person's mind is immediately whisked away to a place of lack, and the trap begins. A downward spiral is inevitable when you begin to secretly covet the life, accomplishments, and relationships that you see around you. I have been guilty of this plenty of times—that is, until God vetoed my plans.

I tried to create movie moments while I was in a long and enduring relationship with someone who is a friend of mine to this day. I was convinced that I could have what I saw on television, on Facebook, and read in books. Soon, I realized that life and especially relationships didn't work that way. What can I say? I was young. I didn't know then what I know now.

I tried to get my boyfriend to go to the park with me, which wasn't exactly his favorite thing to do. On one particular occasion, I had planned a park day for the two of us, and It didn't go as planned. That's strange! I sat at the park alone, angry and frustrated. I was really upset that he was not excited to go to the park. His attitude was, "I'll go because you want me to go, but if I had it my way, we wouldn't be going." That's the response that I received, so I went to the park alone.

Later, I was informed that he had convinced himself that it wouldn't be so bad to just come, being that he knew I would be thrilled for him to do so. But it was too late. Miracle's mind was made up, and when Miracle's mind is made up, there is no stopping her. So I sat at Highland Park, eating my hoagie from Vento's, fuming. I can laugh at it now because it was about six years ago, but back then, it was no laughing matter. I created ideas to live out what I saw take place in the lives of others, and I got to the place where I was not content doing it alone because in many ways, my entire life had been lived that way.

The challenge in not being content or confident in who you are and your own presence is that you start to look for people to fill areas of your life that they aren't capable of filling. They may try with everything within them, but the truth remains. That's not their role in your life. What I tried to use as personal fulfillment was a relationship, but for you, it may be a job that you have tried to squeeze into your life and it just hasn't worked. The only result you gain in doing this is frustration, which ultimately leads to nothing good.

About two years ago, I realized what I had done while I was in the relationship. I also was able to identify expectations that were in place due to my eyes being on what others had. Your life was meant to be lived by you, through you, and for you.

Life was never meant to be lived through the lives of other people. In fact, the reason most people lack contentment in themselves is because they have not spent enough time alone with themselves. In order to find a proper and healthy sense of contentment in yourself, you actually have to spend time with yourself. You would be surprised what you can learn about yourself alone. It's something that I have found to be a defining tool in understanding where I am and where I am going.

I am very serious and take major pride in my walks in the park these days. I bask in the presence of my King (God) and enjoy the sun beaming down on what I refer to as my park blanket. I enjoy life. There was a time in my life when I couldn't fathom going to the park alone. I felt that I needed to have someone there with me to create a moment. How hilarious is that? When you live life with limits, you will try all sorts of things. However, once you embrace the fact that God has vetoed your plan and the moments you tried to create, you begin to open up to the possibility and truth of there being a better way.

Contentment was a characteristic in my life that was definitely lacking. Sure, I traveled, preached, and encountered many different people. I was both blessed and humbled with an amazing life; but I also have moments when God has to remind me that life is not about what was or what's next but what is. This reminder always put me back on track.

I am constantly able to identify the fact that my past only has the relevance that I allot to it and that which I choose to share. My future only has as much potential as I am willing to pursue. I went from being a discontented, pouting girlfriend some years ago to a very content and vibrant single woman who delights in moments with the King, enjoys dinners alone, treats herself to movies, buys beautiful flowers that remind her of the beauty of life, and spends the majority of her summer afternoons at the park.

A person can decide whether he or she wants to create moments or become the moments that he or she looks to create. I've chosen to no longer participate in the former way of things but to embrace life for every moment that is created by me just because I am present. You may have days when you wish you could call up a friend and just vent to him or her about your boss or call up that special someone and just share the joys of your day. However, one of the most valuable lessons that can be learned in life concerning support is that you are able to get it from whoever is always present, and outside of God, that person is you—the audience of one.

Maybe you were like me, waiting to create moments and finding yourself frustrated by the inability to produce your grand idea. Maybe you worked hard to get to where you are in life right now, but you don't quite understand why you've had to do it alone. Maybe you have been married for some years and have been challenged with not being able to have children. Whatever season you may be in or want to be in, know what is meant to be will be, and what will be will not escape you.

You don't have to chase, force, question, or worry about a relationship. For the time being, learn to live in, embrace, and love the present because all you have is right now.

## CHAPTER 14

# Sink or Swim

*In life, there are those who drown in disappointment and those who learn to swim using disappointment as a life jacket.*

A life jacket is used to keep one above water, especially in cases where the person has a limited ability to swim. However, in life, there are many people who have never been taught to swim or truly live life to the fullest. One might argue that it is impossible to teach someone to truly live. I disagree. The experiences that you welcome in your life can become your greatest teacher.

Based on my own relational experiences, I learned quite a bit about life, contentment, and what it means to live in the present. I learned a lesson or two concerning how to maintain a healthy relationship as well as a healthy life. This not only proves, but also gives a point of reference concerning various ways in which one can be taught a thing or two about living. Life is not only what you make of it, but also what you allow. Your life can become limited not only by what you make of it, but also by what you allow in it.

On the other hand, we have the ability to pick and choose what we allow to change us—for better or worse. At any given moment, you have the ability to either allow the disappointments that you've experienced in life make you better or make you bitter. This is

## WHEN GOD VETOES YOUR PLAN

what we classify as being the sink or swim response. Many become accustomed to allowing life's disappointments to drown them. Some learn the importance and value of disappointment and use it as a life jacket to keep above water. There is no doubt that being able to look at disappointments in life as valuable defining factors is a very hard thing to do. However, in order to stay above water, it is a must.

Recently, I planned a trip to Jamaica with one of my girlfriends. We were both excited, and I was one day away from purchasing the ticket. I woke up that morning and signed in on the website. To my surprise, the package went up over $300—talk about being disappointed. It was going to be a short trip, and for the initial, all-inclusive price that was offered, we figured we'd be crazy to pass it up. However, once the priced increased, we no longer had interest. I had already marked the dates in my little black planner and envisioned myself in Jamaica. What I learned about disappointment that day is that though you can't escape it, you certainly can change your response to it.

Maybe your current response is that you were never taught to swim by living life to the fullest. However, no matter how true that might have been, what's stopping you from learning now? Many people will become content in what they don't know, and when life's disappointments begin to drown them, the response is, "No one ever taught me" when really, the truth is there was never a desire to know. We keep certain lessons in life on a need-to-know basis. If it's not relevant for something now, then we feel that we don't need to know. Unfortunately, this mentality will leave you out in the deep, stranded with no help in sight—all because it seemed irrelevant at the time.

Situations change quickly. Every lesson in life is worth learning, whether it is considered needed for today or useful for tomorrow. Don't allow your eyes to be closed to the possibility of new opportunities or become disillusioned by what didn't work out. There will always be another day and a better way. You have the ability to make use of every experience in your life as a floating device that keeps you on top of things—or you can consistently drown in what didn't work out.

You are invited to live a life in which disappointments take on a new form and challenges are welcomed because of all that is produced as a result. There's not much that you can experience in this life without limits that will leave you out in the deep end, fending for your life. However, what will leave you in the deep is your refusal to use the life jacket that is provided. Sink or swim—the choice is yours—but the life that God invites you to provides you with all that you need, including your life jacket. God has the ability to use every situation in our lives to work out for our good—even the disappointments. The question is this: will you?

## CHAPTER 15

# Pack Light

*Where are you going with all that stuff?*

Have you ever seen the suitcases that some people take on three- to four-day trips? What do they have in there, and what do they plan to do with all of those clothes? I have learned the essence of "less is more," and I ran with it! I used to be like most women, packing at least five to seven pairs of shoes and who knows how many pieces of jewelry to match every outfit. The amount of clothes compressed into the suitcase would be just as unnecessary to pack as it is to discuss. After moving for the second time out of the United States, I've learned a thing or two concerning what it means to pack light.

You have probably done what I've done in the past—stand at the desk in the airport, holding your breath as you place your gigantic suitcase on the scale. I knew when I lifted the suitcase that I had put way too much stuff in it and that it would definitely be overweight. I waited to hear, "Ma'am, you will need to remove a few items or pay extra to take it with you." Surprisingly, there were occasions when I was able to slide through and have a heavy tag. I was extremely grateful on those occasions. After a while, I figured it out—pack light.

Life is much like what we place in our suitcases. We recognize what we need; yet we pack what we need and all that we want as well. I am the first to say that God blesses us with needs and wants.

However, it is all in perspective. Unlike our suitcases, we rarely have someone tell us that we have too many things packed into our lives. Very seldom are we charged a fee or even asked to remove things from our lives by coworkers, friends, or family. But somewhere down the line, we begin to feel the weight of what we've packed. We also fail to make note of the fact that we continue to add a few more suitcases so that we can take everything.

What started off as a three- to four-day trip turned in to a lifetime of commitments to people, jobs, and relationships that we had no room for. Be honest—you knew when you took that second job that your time was already stretched thin, and then you actually started to question why you felt worn out. You knew when the woman said she was not ready to settle down what you were in for, but you just couldn't get past those lips and hips. You knew when he didn't return any of your calls that he had used you for what he wanted and was done. However, with all of the facts before you, you were blind—willingly blind.

Your suitcases (life) are beginning to tear. They are falling apart at the seams, and for some strange reason, you are convinced that you can keep everything in them and fix the suitcase all at the same time. Just stop and look around; things are falling out of your suitcase. You left a trail behind you, but because you took on that second job, enrolled in the gym, and became the coach for your daughter's basketball team, you didn't even notice.

It's time to unpack. It's time to evaluate where you are going, what you need to bring, and how long you will be there. Until your plan becomes vetoed by God, you don't actually begin to see how stuck and limited you were in your plan and the life you lived. You don't need three suitcases on this journey. All you need is to carry on.

## CHAPTER 16

## Carry On

*The ability to move on when life wants
to hold you back is a precious gift.*

I often wonder how I managed to carry on with life when everything worked against me. I came to the conclusion that it wasn't me who managed to carry on with life; it was life that managed to carry on with me. There is a difference between allowing what you've experienced to take over your life and letting your life take over what you experience.

Experiences play a role in our lives, and we must also discuss the role our lives have in relation to our experiences. The way you view your life is based on your state of mind, causing everything about your life to follow suit. That pattern often identifies key aspects of your life as far as where you work, how you work, if you are normally punctual or late, whether you begin projects and finish them, or whether you move from one project to the next without completing any.

The ability to move forward when your life tries to hold you back is due to a specific state of mind that is fashioned in determination and passion. It is imperative that one is both determined and passionate about that which is pursued in life. If a person is passionate but not determined, he or she may start off strong but at some point lose hope because of adversity. If a person is determined but not passionate, he or she will stay the course but become miserable in accomplishing a goal because the heart is not in it. Do you see now how the two work together and must stay together?

My experiences in life were challenging at times. However, knowing that in the same moment I allow those experiences to take over my life, is the same moment I that I become defeated. One who believes in himself or herself to accomplish great things lives a life that has the ability to keep moving and progress against all odds. Odds were stacked against me, but there was also greatness in the distance that I could actually see. Often, the silver lining ahead that becomes visible in one's life can be the very thing that gives hope to continue. In essence, you start living to live. You become motivated to motivate.

When people become the essence of what they are created to do, they stop looking for reasons to carry on because the defining factor of who they are is that they never stop, quit, or take breaks. You don't have to defend the existence of something when it is living and active right before your eyes. What is there to defend—the reality of what you see or the fact that you actually believe what is before you? In this way, life is presented to us by God. He saw lifelessness—lives that went from day to day, creating plans that were limited to possibility, resources, and often finances. He knew that something had to be done to stop you from cyclical thinking, so He decided to veto your plan.

At that moment, you didn't find it to be fair. In fact, you were enraged by the idea that God, who wants good things for you, would get in the way of all your good plans. However, the reason your plan was vetoed was to expose you to the lie of limitation that you functioned with the entire time. There is no way that you would have the ability to carry on with your plan, because your experiences would have swallowed you up (taken over your life). As soon as your plan failed to work, you would have been lost, but God stepped in vetoed your plan.

God presented to you His plan and actually left the choice up to you. That decision is still in your hands. You can take all the time you need, but recognize that the more time you take, the more you prolong the immediate joy and satisfaction that come along with this new life.

## WHEN GOD VETOES YOUR PLAN

There was a man in the Bible named Joseph who received a dream concerning the plan that God had for His life. However, his family members did not agree with his dream. To make matters worse, he gave them all the details about the dream, causing jealousy to rise to the surface. His brothers were so angry that they came up with a plan of their own to actually kill him. They were not too fond of him. However, instead of killing him, they altered their plan a bit and decided to sell him, later telling their father that a wild animal had eaten him! They didn't know that their selling of him was God vetoing their plan and preparing to use every experience that Joseph had to bring him closer to his dream.

The essence of this account is that no matter what experiences we have, there is a state of mind that can push us toward success or lead us straight to defeat. For over a decade, Joseph had experiences that had the potential to strip him of everything that he once believed, much like your experiences. I can only imagine that Joseph believed more in what he saw in that dream than what he experienced day to day. He was convinced. He is a perfect example of one who refused to allow experiences to take over his life. He was determined to have life take over, shape, alter, and endure every experience.

This mentality is that of a winner. Do you know when a person becomes a winner? Is it when the medal is around his or her neck or at the moment the person begins to train, removing all possibilities of defeat or failure? The mentality of a winner is that of one who does not let life pass him or her by but one whose life tries to catch up with every idea, dream, and aspiration.

It is now day three of writing. Initially, I gave myself ten days to start and finish this book. However, I am certain that I will be finished tomorrow. Within four days, this book will be created and finished. How does that happen? With God, of course, but also with a mind-set that refuses to let life pass by. I have no doubt that my very being wonders what in the world I am doing and why. But God is clearly doing the writing, so there is no doubt in my mind that at this moment, this is what I've been created to do—let Him lead.

Let's adopt the mentality of winners. If a winner becomes the winner at the moment he or she removes not just the possibility, but also the existence of defeat, than what does that tell us about life? We have the ability to create what we want; we also have the ability to destroy that which we were created to do. We can live in the existence of what we believe before it actually happens. We came to the agreement that the winner became the winner not after the medal was placed around his or her neck but at the moment the winner saw the medal and made a decision to remove the existence of defeat. There are decisions that we make from the beginning that identify if we will win or lose.

These key factors concerning the life of a winner not only help us to understand the state of mind of a winner, but also give us guidelines concerning how we view our own lives. Have you ever seen a mob of people form a circle to see a fight take place? If you have, you also know that there comes a point in every fight where an adult will step in, break up the fight, and tell the mob of people, "Carry on; there's nothing to see here." Does this sound familiar? Our experiences tend to follow this same format. There have been experiences in your life that drew crowds of people. However, not too much later, someone comes or something happens that causes that crowd to disperse. There is nothing more to see.

What does this have to do with being able to carry on? It has absolutely everything to do with having the strength, courage, and confidence to carry on. In fact, if you don't know when there is nothing more to see, you will be left standing in what was, never realizing that it is no more. In order to carry on, you must live with your eyes open. You must realize that the experience that once cost you everything is over, the job that you were fired from no longer exists, the car that you loved has been repossessed, and the person you gave your heart to gave it back. This is your chance to carry on, pack light, and stop allowing your past experiences keep you from moving on. There is nothing left. Everyone is gone, and you are the only one still standing there, looking at what was and trying to make sense of it.

When God vetoes your plan, He says, "Carry on; there is nothing more to see here."

# CHAPTER 17

## *Fear Came Knocking*

*I've never been one for horror movies. I find no point in them. There are enough occurrences in life that place fear in our hearts as it is.*

Not long ago, I received a phone call that would shatter my perception of life—one that was quite limited, to say the least. I was sitting outside of one of the local colleges in Prince George, waiting for a friend, when my phone rang. My grandma was returning my call, but I could barely understand anything she said in between her weeping and trying to explain to me what was going on. I quickly learned that she had received a phone call from the doctors, and the report was not good. She had recently had an MRI because of recurring headaches, and the doctor called to report the results—a brain tumor.

My heart instantly sank, and I felt sick to my stomach. However, I remained calm and strong for her as she shared as much as she could. She was so overcome by emotion that she had to get off the phone. As soon as the phone read "call ended," I began to weep. How could this happen? This was impossible.

Words do not covey the fear that entered my heart and mind at the thought of losing her. I immediately called Pastor Paul, and he gave comforting words, ensuring that whatever I needed was available. I felt like I was in a fog. It was one of the most surreal moments in my life. What would I do if something happened to her? We talked on the phone a minimum of three times a day. She knows how to Skype and recently started texting me. This could not be happening. It took about a day for me to come back to earth because I was definitely not present.

I have not experienced many deaths in my family, so for the most part, I don't know what it's like to lose someone who is extremely close. In 2012, Bishop Otis Lockett passed away, a man who I admired, honored, and looked up to. When I found out the news of his passing, I was so overwhelmed that I didn't know what to do. I was in complete shock, and even my response to his death shocked me. During that time, the thought of grandma passing at some point was fleeting, but now it came knocking at my door.

Time passed, and many prayers flooded the heavens on my grandma's behalf. Prayer chains went up throughout the city of Pittsburgh as well as Prince George. I sensed that fear came knocking at my door, but that didn't mean I had to let it in. A few weeks later, another appointment was scheduled. On that day, all of our fears were removed in an instant. The tumor was not on her brain but the lining of the skin. Surgery was not needed, and her headaches were a result of arthritis in her neck and spine. I could sense over the phone that grandma was back to her old self again. Fear came knocking, and when we peeped through the window to identify it, it was gone.

However, during this time, there were lies that I believed—lies that once again reflected areas in my life that were still bound by limits. When I first received the news, I began to fear that I wouldn't be able to cope with life and be miserable and lonely. The fact that my grandma and I talk on the phone at least three times a day was a huge gap for someone to fill, and up to that point, I had not imagined being married or the possibility of having children without Grandma. I realized that I had lived my life limiting God being everything to me. He used Grandma throughout the years to reflect His love for me. Quickly, I was reminded that at the end of the day, all of my fountains are in Him. Everything that gives me life is provided by God.

This does not mean that at the point when our loved ones are no longer with us on earth that we won't experience grief because we will. However, the promise that we have in this life is that joy comes in the midst of sorrow, and voids are filled in ways that can't be tangibly seen. This is the promise that we have in God. Though fear comes knocking at the door, greater is the strength that lives at the door of our hearts to overcome it all. Refuse to believe the lies that you will never be able to move on because your loved one passed, having been without work for over a year, or feelings of insecurity concerning your worth and value.

When a loved one who has been life for you passes away, in many ways, God is saying your plan to depend on that person for the rest of your life has been vetoed. God will take over from there and provide needed comfort. The gifts of memories and moments in time that you've been able to share will be like a locket that one wears around the neck—a treasure that is far greater than what the eye can see.

Fear will come knocking, but that doesn't mean you need to answer the door. You are too busy catering to that which gives you life.

## CHAPTER 18

# The Journey

*My mentor once asked, "Miracle, what if life was not about the final destination but the journey? What if life was meant to be revealed through every pitfall and pit stop along the way? Would you then view your journey differently?"*

Life has a way of throwing curve balls at you unexpectedly. You could either always be ready to duck or be hit by what's coming. The first option keeps your eyes open and mind alert at all times, while the other allows you to live for the moment and enjoy all that comes. I'd like to think that the proper response is not either or but both. As you explore the meaning of your life, you must be aware that getting hit every once in a while by the unexpected is not necessarily a bad thing. In fact, unexpected situations reveal to us just how prepared we are for life.

Living without limits means there will be things that occur that are unimaginable, meaning there was no way of telling that they would happen. However, you can live life understanding that anything is possible at any given time. This way of thinking does not ensure that you will not have moments when you are shocked by news or even blown away by a surprise. What begins to happen is that you create a mentality that looks at life through a kaleidoscope of limitless possibilities, options, and outcomes.

# WHEN GOD VETOES YOUR PLAN

This mentality allows you to see beauty in all things, which is gift. Many people spend their entire lives missing out on the beauty of the seasons that they are in by wishing they were in other seasons of life. Do not to rob yourself of what was created to place a smile on your face.

During my time in the Caribbean, God said, "Miracle, do you really believe that I would send you all the way to the Virgin Islands to be unhappy? I've sent you here to not only train you, but also show you the beauty of this season of your life." I asked God for forgiveness and to change my attitude. Your attitude changes when everything you know has been far removed and that which you try to hang on to seems to slip through your fingers. God used the Virgin Islands to teach me some valuable lessons about life, love, God, people, and honesty.

I was fresh out of college, living in St. Croix. My family and friends were in shock and could not believe that I was moving so far away. However, just as in every other decision, I felt peace and assurance. I will never forget flying over Puerto Rico, bawling my eyes out. It hit me that I had actually moved away from Pittsburgh. This was not a vacation trip; this would be my new home. The man sitting next to me on the plane didn't speak English, so he motioned to the attendant for a beverage for me. He must have thought, *This girl is losing it!* I was thankful and responded with, "Gracias."

I got to my place and saw all of my boxes there. Overwhelmed by the reality of my new life, I said aloud, "You really did it. You live here. What are you thinking?" I then plopped down on my bed and smiled. I knew from that day forward that my journey on the less-traveled path had begun. There was no thought put into moving to the Virgin Islands. From the moment I stepped off the plane for the interview, I knew that I would soon call it home. There was no thinking concerning a decision like this.

We often think ourselves out of blessings, because we are comfortable with familiarity and aren't willing to step out into the unknown. This is the life you are invited to live. What is there to think about? Did I like the weather, was I okay with geckos, was I prepared to live on my own in culture that was different from my own, or would the people at the church accept me? I consider those questions to be irrelevant.

Most of the questions that we ask along the journey are irrelevant. However, we become so used to wanting to be in control that we lose sight of the fact that this life has no limits or plans. You can end up doing anything, anywhere—and as long as God has sent me and is there with me, I'm okay with it. The sad thing is that for most of us, that's not enough. How we get to a place of depending on everyone and everything more than God is scary to me. It is my hope that as you read this book, you begin to lean on and trust God more than ever.

My time in the Caribbean taught me more about myself than I could have ever imagined. That is because of what I gained there. You never know how strong you are until a challenge comes. The greatest challenge that anyone can experience in this life is being placed in leadership. It doesn't matter if it's in the church or corporate America. Your ability to properly lead others will define you as a leader. St. Croix taught me the importance of staying before God's presence and trusting that whatever people need, He will use you to provide, no matter how incapable you think you are.

On many occasions, I asked God to teach me how to lead the youth and become selfless. I felt inadequate, even with all that I had accomplished throughout my teen years and time in college, interning at the jail in Pittsburgh, and speaking at juvenile facilities. Leading the youth as a Pastor was not the same. I wasn't able to put my finger on what made me feel that way until I realized that God wanted me to no longer lead based on what I had done or learned in the past. He wanted me to put my heart into it, to not just be a presence in the lives of the youth but to actually be part of their lives. Once I began to build relationships, I began to understand.

There were women in St. Croix who adopted me as a daughter with whom I am still very close. In moments when I felt alone on the journey, God sent these women to come by the office just to visit, bring me a meal, or say hello. God used them as angels in my life.

Until now, I have never shared the loneliness that I experienced while embarking upon one of the greatest assignments in my life. I believe that it needs to be acknowledged. Saying "Yes" to God often means saying no to what looks normal (whatever that means).

The relationships that I built with the youth in St. Croix compare to none. It was the first time that I experienced transformation taking place right before my eyes. I watched youth who were once quiet stand before their peers and lead. I watched youth who had no desire to be expressive about their faith call me with excitement that they led someone to Christ. I have even watched youth experience the presence of God in a way that changed their lives instantly. Some of these youth minister, some are university students, and some have even decided to dedicate their life to missions. Was it worth it? Absolutely!

I attribute everything I know concerning behind-the-scenes ministry work to Victorious Believers Ministries. Senior Pastor Reginald Perry was the first leader who gave me the opportunity to lead the people God had entrusted to him, and for that I am forever thankful. My prayer life skyrocketed, administrative skills developed, and the importance of trusting God above everything became the theme of my life there. St. Croix was certainly preparation for Canada, and I have no idea what Canada is preparing me for. The love and warmth that I am able to experience on a day-to-day basis compare to none.

Consider all that has taken place in your life up to this point. Can you imagine being the person you are today without those experiences? There have been aspects of the journey that you wish you could have bypassed, but can you honestly say that any of it was pointless? Of course not.

The path that you are on will lead to various people, places, and things. However, your willingness to accept the beauty of that path enables you to enjoy the journey. There are scenarios in life that you thought you would never laugh about, but you are amazed that you can. Why is that? Could it be that you realized that it wasn't as bad as it could have been? Or maybe it was really bad, but you can laugh now because you never thought you would get over it. You thought that it was the end of you! I can recall situations like that!

The good news is that every pitfall and pit stop brings you closer to the final destination. Although life is about the journey, there would be no destination if there were no path to be taken. Embrace the journey that you are on. Don't worry about who isn't with you or is on the way. Carry on, and keep moving forward. Your journey awaits you. Life awaits you.

I know you have been rerouted a few times due to your plans being vetoed by God. If God had not vetoed your plans, you would be at a dead end right now. Let's not talk about all of the accidents along the way. Let's just focus on the fact that you would have been at a dead end by now, hoping that someone would come along who could give you directions. Be thankful. God saved you from being stranded out in the middle of nowhere.

During the journey, you will often experience minor roadblocks. Most of the roadblocks will be you. Don't worry. We all have a tendency from time to time to get in our own way. However, the closer you get to the roadblocks, the more you will notice that they begin to disappear. This is the part of the journey where you become less like you and more like God. Therefore, no longer be a hindrance to yourself but a help.

**Needed items for the journey:**

1. *An Open Mind* Most of what God will reveal to you along the way will be different from what you are used to. Being closed off to that which is unknown will get you nowhere, so remain open to new insight. You don't know it all. In actuality, you know very little.
2. *Passion and Determination* You will need both—especially to get you through the days when the pitfalls seem deep and almost impossible to get out of.

3. *Confidence* Many people will tell you what you can't do. At moments, you will be tempted to believe them, but you must remain confident in who and whose you are.
4. *Contentment* Having some soft spots is a part of the journey. But you are on a journey; your current location is not permanent.
5. *Love* It is imperative that you grow to love your journey—even the pitfalls that you wish could have been avoided. This is not an overnight process. However, it will happen to the extent you desire. My personal love relationship with my journey did not happen overnight, but when I realized that I was in for the time of my life, I grew to love it in a hurry!

Throughout your journey, you will experience moments when you miss the things of your past. The only relevance your past has is that which you give it. Often, we long for the things of our past only to find what we really long for is complete wholeness and a life that can break free from cyclical thinking. The truth of the matter is that what you had or who you used to be wasn't that great, and the fact that you are in a transition taints your view of that.

Have you ever seen someone from your past who you were involved with and wondered what you saw in him or her from the beginning? I'm sure you have. There are moments in all of our lives when decisions are made out of a place of lack rather than what we actually need.

There are days when I need to eat a meal of good substance, but instead, I will grab some chips, a granola bar, and some sushi and call it a day. I needed to eat a meal that was a lot better than what I chose. However, I took whatever was available. We often treat our journey in life the same way, knowing what we need to get closer to our final destination but choosing what's easy and fast. The result of making that decision will indeed take you a few steps back. It's important to make decisions after you are able to be honest with yourself concerning what you want. On any given day, I am liable to have horrible eating habits; however, I recognize that those decisions will catch up to me.

On any given day, you may liable to pick your phone up and welcome the person back into your life putting you a few steps back along your journey. Furthermore, that person didn't support your journey from the beginning. How often in life do we seek aspirations, people, jobs, or attainment from a place of lack rather than actual need? The difference between a void in your life and a need is that a void will cause you to search in all the wrong places to temporarily fill it, whereas a need can only be filled by that which it longs for; artificial filler won't do. The need will remain, and the void will continually get filled by that which is temporary.

There may be a void in your life due to you not having a father or mother. That void in your life lacks love, acceptance, appreciation, and everything else that comes along with a parent. Instead of taking care of the need—having a parent or seeking out a mentor—you may begin to fill the void with relationships. The void in your life caused you to respond in a way that sought after artificial fillers while the need remained. It was not your plan to have parents who neglected you, a job that would no longer need you, and a child who would end up going in a downward spiral. However, God is able to take what wasn't your plan and use it for His. He knew that there would be struggles and hardships, but He also knew that He would have the perfect solution.

Your journey will cause many bumps and bruises along the way, but I think of them as beauty marks. In our hurts, we experience the greatest season of healing, and in our aloneness, we receive the greatest season of comfort. Being able to understand what season you are in can help you to identify the route that you should take. Many times, we get lost because we have no idea what season we are in. This happens more often than not. When you become complacent where you are, you lose sight of where you are going.

You are on a journey, which means your life will never be stagnant. If ever there is a time when your life becomes stagnant, it's because you've stopped moving. It is challenging to know that you have potential to go so far but choose not to take another step. In the Bible, people heard that there would be a prophet whose name would be Jesus the Christ. However, when He showed up on the scene, they denied that it was Him. With all of the facts, miracles, and prophecies, they chose not to believe.

Along the journey, we will be tempted to do the same exact thing—see the potential that lives inside of us, know for sure that it exists, but dismiss the possibility willingly. Could it be that to acknowledge what is there would require a level of responsibility? Could it be that to accept the fact that there is potential to be whatever you want would no longer allow you any excuse? Could it be that having the ability to succeed against all odds is frightening because up to this point, it is unknown territory?

You are invited to live life through a kaleidoscope. No matter which way you turn, there will be beauty before you. You may look forward to the day when you can retire, enjoy grandchildren, take vacations when you want, and buy the car that your spouse says is unnecessary. However, there is a clear path that needs to be taken, and that clear path will not come without pitfalls and pit stops along the way. It's God's way of saying, "Here comes a curve ball; either duck or be ready to be hit by life because this is a part of the journey."

# CHAPTER 19

## This Is Temporary

> *Most people become worried by circumstances that are out of their control. I like to tell those people, "Don't worry; this is temporary."*

At one point in my life, I worried about everything. I had a really bad habit of biting my nails. The habit was so bad that I would bite them and not even know it. My parents are very important to me, and although the restoration and healing process that we have experienced has taken place over the past five years, when I was a child, they caused my worry.

I had a relationship with God at a really young age. I was about five when I started to pray for hours. I even had a crochet door hanger that read, "*Shhhh*, I'm talking to God." I spent a lot of time with God in prayer, and most of my prayers were directed toward my family. There were even nights when I had dreams about them.

On countless occasions, I called my family into the living room after a time of prayer and had a family discussion. I was about seven years old when this began. My household included my mom, Grandma, Uncle Wayne, and Uncle Romie (Jerome). My grandma helped me get everyone up because most of the time, everyone had already gone to bed. I shared with them what God said to me. Most of the time, the talks consisted of me saying, "You all need to get your lives together. God wants a relationship with you all, and you have to stop what you are doing. Don't you know that He loves you?"

I went on for quite some time, and if any of them parted their lips to say anything out of the way, Grandma said, "Now, you all sit here and listen to this girl. She has more sense than all of you put together." I can remember it like it was yesterday. I was just a child, but my heart ached for my family. My desire for them to know God was a burning passion. I'm the only niece as well as an only child and the only grandchild, so my uncles loved me dearly, even in the late hours of the night. Even to this day, when I travel back to my home in Pittsburgh, my uncles make sure that things are in order.

Since I was a child, I had a mantle of leadership that only God could give. What did I know about leading a family or evangelizing to drug dealers? I was convinced even then that God wanted my life, and I was determined to make sure He had it. I was determined to say whatever He wanted me to say, and it didn't matter to what extent. However, in my heart and passion for God and prayer, I remained worried and often afraid.

When things became increasingly bad with my mom's addiction, I felt like giving up on praying. I spent thirteen years in prayer at that point, and things did not get any better. Grandma made my mother move into her own place, which was a recurring cycle. Her actions were a bit uncontrollable. However, with her education in nursing, she managed to get employment. It was inconsistent, but she could always find work.

I felt lost concerning my calling during this time. I couldn't understand how and why God would use me when things were so messed up at home. In fact, there were days when I felt like I should no longer preach because I couldn't help my family. The only one in my household with a relationship with God was Grandma. At times, I know she must have struggled with where she went wrong. On the other hand, we learn that the decisions people make in their lives rarely have anything to do with other people; most of the time, decisions are the result of an inward battle of the mind.

I prayed during this time in frustration, expressing to God that I was tired of praying. I was in college at this point and had dated for a few years. I thought I wanted to be married, dealt with family struggles, and was unsure about everything else. I knew that I needed God to help me with pretty much everything. I kept telling myself that this season would pass and that it was only temporary, but it became hard to believe that it was temporary after thirteen years. Near my breaking point, God not only blew me away, but also sent a surprise. It was my dad. Much time had passed since I had seen him, but his time of arrival couldn't have been more perfect; little did I know that God had worked on my dad's heart.

At this point, my parents were separated for seventeen years. I never imagined what would take place. They got back together, and my mom relocated to Buffalo, New York, where I was born. My mom knew that change needed to take place, and because my dad made changes in his life, he felt like he could help her. He told Grandma and me that he missed Mommy and wanted to get back with her. Can you believe it? Seventeen years passed, and he came back for her. There are no limits to what God can do. For those of you who feel like there is no hope, there is.

Life has twisted and turned since then, but the fact that my father came for her after all of those years speaks volumes concerning hope. We are told quite often that there is no hope for certain people or after making certain decisions. However, I believe that there is hope as long as there is someone who is willing. My mom's life was forever changed as a result of various things that took place since then. Hopeless situations do not exist, but unwilling people do. The decision made at that point in Mom's life played a major role in her continual journey to freedom. She would also agree that her journey to freedom has not always been easy, but her journey belongs to her as she allows God to show her who she really is. What a warrior I have in that woman!

Worrying about what you have no control over will never help you or the situation. However, praying that God sends a reflection of hope will. Nothing is ever lost for good when someone is willing to set out on a search. When God vetoed your plans, He paved the way for you to search for your real life—the life that belongs to you and is often hidden or suppressed by doubt. This whole time, you thought that God was unlocking doors for you. You are mistaken. He is leading you along the journey so that you can find the keys that unlock those doors.

Have you ever lost your house or car keys? You search frantically, practically tearing the room apart, only to find that the keys are in your pocket. In many ways, our lives are like lost keys. We go about our days without them and don't go searching for them unless we need them. Your life has been lost on many occasions. Sure, you have gone about your day, living in the roles that you were given, whether businessman, doctor, teacher, father, mother, wife, or neighbor, taking care of everything and everyone but you. You look around and realize you are completely lost.

You allowed what you were doing to identify who you were, and at the end of the day, when you are left alone with your thoughts, you have no idea who you are or what your life is all about. You never noticed that this whole time, you lived for a moment, person, goal, or favorable outcome. You've lost the meaning of your life, and as you frantically go searching, you realize that you have no clue as to where you should start. This could be a long process. How do you begin the search for those types of keys? They could be anywhere.

Because you are on a journey, you can't be bombarded with tons of possibilities that are temporary. What do you do? Where do you start? Go back to the place you were mentally before all of these other factors came to be. It takes a moment of self-reflective inventory. Who were you before that company hired you, you welcomed a little life into the world, or the car accident? Can you remember? Do you recall your dreams, life, personal convictions, or questions that weighed heavily on your heart?

The process of reflective inventory requires you to mentally veto all that is in your life that has potential to become temporary. I am not saying those things or people do not have worth and value, because they certainly do. Some have shaped you into who you are today. However, just because something or someone has played a role in your process of being shaped into who you are, that does not mean that they make you who you are. You are who you are, with or without them.

When fear came knocking, I had to take a step back and take a moment of inventory. I had allowed the role that my grandma had played in shaping me into who I am lead me to believe that I could not be without her. No matter how much I want to place her in a place of high esteem, the truth of the matter is that life starts and finishes with the Creator. There is no way around it. The love that I have received from my grandma has been amazing, but when fear came knocking, reality set in that her time on earth is temporary. This led me to take an introspective look at who I am without her physical presence. In this same way, we must recognize the reality of the temporary roles we have or are part of.

Don't allow your life to become lost by temporary hats that you wore, because at some point, you will go looking for your life only to find that it has been stuffed in your pocket. You have the ability to live life without limits; you just have to stop limiting everything that you are capable of.

Today is day four of writing this book. Today, I will complete this book. I recognize that I have the ability to do that which I am willing to pursue. Life is no different with you. We may share different dreams and aspirations, but we both have the ability to not miss the everlasting hope of life without limits by refusing to live our lives based on what is temporary.

I challenge you to think of every role that you have. Do you have your mental list? Now search out who you are without the list. Underneath the long list that identifies you is the real you and the real life that you were created to live. Choose right now to start living above and beyond the list. The people in your life deserve to see who you really are!

# CHAPTER 20

## Ms. Independent

*There is a lot to be said for the one who wants to do everything himself or herself.*

My personality is interesting to almost everyone who I encounter. This is not because I am extremely exciting but because on one end of the spectrum, I am extremely introverted, and on the other end, I am rather extroverted. I am passionate about God, family, life, food, meeting new people, the park, and capturing candid moments with my camera. However, as much as I thoroughly enjoy meeting new people, you will almost never see me approach a group. I'm actually quite shy. You may think that because I've preached before, you don't know how in the world I could ever be shy. I told you, I have a very interesting personality.

On top of being quite introverted, I am also quite independent. By this point, you have read quite a bit about this vetoed life of mine and have more than likely made some observations of your own. Only children and the firstborn can probably relate with me in this. I've been around lots of people, and as much as I love it, I have great appreciation for my alone time with the King at the park or working out and watching a movie on Netflix. Because I was the only child, I didn't have to share anything, and when friends came over, I was very particular about all of the Barbies being in one place and everything being in order. I was a little trip back then. I'll have to ask my childhood friends if they think I had control issues as a child!

I was always the smallest and youngest out of the group, but it didn't seem to bother my friends or me. As children, we made up dance steps in the middle of the street. You couldn't tell us anything; we just knew we were big-time. At one point, we even created a video to be entered into a competition to meet Michael Jackson. Those were the days. However, there were days when we worked on dance moves that I knew in my mind were not appropriate. When I refused to do certain dance moves, I was called stiff. Although I was very young, I knew that I couldn't follow their lead. My mind was made up.

I have no doubt that I was born to lead. In fact, when I was born three months premature and weighing 1.6 pounds, the doctors began to speculate concerning my life and the days to come. My mom knew somehow I would make it because when I came out via Caesarean, my fists were balled up. I was ready for life even back then. I've been fighting my way ever since, through every obstacle, prediction concerning my life, and testimony that I have lived to tell. I was born ready to live. In fact, life has tried to catch up to me since day one.

In many ways, I see a common thread as to how life experiences mold and shape us into who we are. I am also aware that having an independent personality and way of thinking in this life can taint and even eliminate a desire or want for support. If you stop looking for or expecting support in your life, you begin to believe that it's not needed. There is another end of the spectrum for people who feel like they can't accomplish anything without someone constantly cheering them on. Knowing that you have support is important and certainly has value, but if you don't have confidence in what you do, the support of others can become a crutch to your success.

One can spend his or her entire life trying to do everything and be everything for everyone. This is indeed an exhausting and limited life. On the other hand, one can recognize that there is a reason why we live in something called a community. It's not by accident that our society does not function with everyone living in his or her own cave. Nothing would get done if we lived this way. Our lives are influenced, and as we discussed in the previous chapter, often identified by the roles we have, often including various people. In knowing this, it's safe to say that people are needed. This is a concept that I used to wrestle with.

Some time ago, I spoke with my mentor concerning the dynamics of needing people. I passionately said that I saw nowhere in the Bible that stated people were needed. I felt that God was needed, of course, and that He used people to accomplish certain things. However, I was not quite sold on the fact that if He did not use people, things would not get done. My mentor then said to me, "Miracle, you are looking at it the wrong way. It's not about if things could still get done. The question is, is that God's original intent as to how things should get done?" He got me.

After having a bit more dialogue concerning the matter of needing people, I soon learned that everything we read in the Bible stems from the roles that we have in a community of people. I was also able to see that all of my questions were irrelevant in reference to God's original plan. We often try to find other means of explanation when the truth is found in the original plan. I allowed my independent thinking to remove the validity of God's original intent. Leave it up to us, and there's no telling what we will convince ourselves of.

I also realized that my personality and ways in which I experienced life played major roles in how I viewed others. My perspective also came from a place of not being able to depend on many people. There were very few constant people in my life, and once I began to relocate, my consistency in their lives changed as well. This is a part of the journey. It is a truth that most of the time we try to ignore. However, when you embrace who you are and what you are called to, nothing else matters.

The truth is that we have all experienced moments in life that we wish could have been shared with others. Whatever the circumstances were, that moment had to be experienced in a personal way. This is not necessarily a bad thing. In fact, everyone should have moments in life when they find complete contentment and joy in who he or she is, just as he or she is, right where he or she is. This is a lesson that must be retaught at various points in one's life. We lose sight of the fact that we came into this world alone, and when we depart, it will be the same.

When I realized that God had vetoed my plans, I also realized that my life would no longer look the same. You are not just welcoming a change of style, taste, scenery, or people. Your life will never look the same. There is no way you can imagine all that is in store, but it is good. God took my want to do everything without asking for help and placed a genuine excitement in my heart for rest!

There are great benefits to understanding where you were, where you are, and where you are created to be. This is part of a process that requires you to get out of the way. I heard a friend once pray, "Lord, have your way; we don't want to be in the way." I thought, *What a prayer. What a selfless thought.* How often can we remember saying "God, have your way" but remaining in His way? God must think we are kind of funny at times.

A heart that is willing to let go of independent ways that get in the way of God is a heart that is open to change. One of the hardest things to do in life is change. This is what postpones almost everything in life. One of the reasons you are invited to a life without limits is because change needs to take place. It wasn't enough for God to veto your plans, because He knew you'd still get in the way. Our willingness to change is interrelated with how we think as well.

Something in our thinking independently from God keeps us in a rut. It's based on the fact that we are created to depend, rely, and lean on God for everything. The scary thing is that many of us have been thinking independently from God for so long that we don't even realize that we do it. This is when God steps in, completely vetoes what we're doing, and offers a solution. However, what is being offered is just that—an offer—an invitation that we are free to accept or decline. Depending on how desperate you are for change, you will either wait it out or accept at that very moment.

Be aware that living life independently from others as well as God will only take you but so far. Giving God not only the way you live, but also the way you think is the beginning of a transformed life. You are on a journey, and for the rest of your days, you will never be alone or led by thoughts that are independent from God. I'm thankful for the lesson learned.

## CHAPTER 21

*Life of Freedom*

*I didn't know I was bound until God freed me.*

I will never forget my day of freedom on February 19, 2011. I was once again at Evangel Fellowship in Greensboro, North Carolina. (Great things take place at that ministry.) I heard about Encounter but had no idea what it was outside of the location and that I was told to be open. I thought to myself, *That shouldn't be too hard. My life is an open book!* Ha, Ha! People told me that major deliverance would take place. I didn't feel like I connected with that aspect of things. After all, I had been in ministry my whole life, and deliverance was definitely not something that I felt I was in need of.

It's interesting how the very thing that you think you don't need often becomes the very thing that makes you wonder how you lived without it. This was certainly my story. I arrived at Encounter and signed in at the desk. The hall was full of women. We were all a bit nervous and had no clue what to expect. Little did we know that God was setting us up to live our best lives yet. I walked in the room and actually felt weak in the knees. There was a sense that God was in the room.

The first night, no one prayed over me. The time of worship was so intense that I didn't know what to do. I asked myself, *Should I stand? Should I sit? Should I kneel? Because God is certainly in the room.*

In an environment like that, one really has no idea what to do. As the night ended, we were all handed two papers. It was a list of every foul thing that a person could ever imagine. We were told to check off everything on the list that we or anyone in our immediate families had been a part of.

At first, I was under the impression that this couldn't be for me. I had never even heard of half of the things on the paper. It didn't take long for me to get through the list, as I was supposed to include my family as well. I went to sleep that night feeling anxious to be free from the things that I had checked off that list once I considered my family. There are often cycles that go from generation to generation, and being able to see it on paper made me a little uncomfortable, to say the least.

For the next two days, I experienced inward transparency like never before. Images flashed before my eyes of things that had happened at least fifteen years ago. Old thoughts, feelings, and desires came out of nowhere. At first, I didn't know what was happening to me, and then I realized that all of these awful things were being brought to the surface because God was preparing to remove them from my life for good. I had major issues in my life that I wasn't even aware of, and during Encounter, there was a freedom that released me from every weight.

My life has not been the same since. I celebrate the fact that God took all of my pride and false sense of humility and completely freed me. A life of freedom awaits you. You can't imagine the joy that oozes from one who has received it. I came back and told everyone; I even discussed it on Facebook and encouraged everyone to go at some point. You may not feel stuck; you may feel like that sort of thing is for someone else. But don't be fooled. There is a life that has no chains or ties to anyone or anything. This life belongs to you.

You deserve to live a life of freedom. Maybe you read this book and said to yourself, "Wow, that's a lot," but a life in God is a life that is free. You were created to live outside of the shadows of every mistake. There is forgiveness, and there is always hope. Are you willing to step out of that box and receive your freedom? Life is not only what you make of it, but also what you allow. Often, we are fooled into thinking that life will be whatever cards are dealt, but I beg to differ. Life is what cards you chose to keep in your hand.

You don't have to accept everything that comes your way, and you don't have to live a life that allows any and everything. You were created with a purpose, and based on your pursuit, it will be manifested. The choice is yours; the ball is in your court. What will you choose? I thought I didn't need to be free from anything or forgive anyone. In my mind, I had let it all go. But I came back from Encounter, picked up my phone, and made a call that erased all pride.

There may be some calls that you need to make. There may be calls that make your stomach drop just at the thought. But there is freedom in your decision to let go of you and welcome God. There is a freedom in releasing everything in your life that you've had a grip on. It's quite liberating. When you welcome every flaw to rise to the surface, you open the door for it to leave.

You are as free as you allow yourself to be. The interesting concept concerning freedom is that it is also a state of mind. When I did my internship at Allegheny County Jail (ACJ) as a chaplain, I said to the inmates during one of the services that freedom is a choice that one makes daily. It's not the bars that keep you incarcerated; it's you state of mind. There are people who are free to do and go as they please, but they stay stuck where they are because their minds are bound.

There are people who make the decision to remain slaves to their own thoughts, fears, and themselves. How does this happen? They are stuck in cyclical thinking. I heard many of the inmates say that they didn't know how to live beyond the bars! What a statement. They testified to the fact that they had no idea how to live a free man's life. You and I are no different.

You may have never been placed in a jail cell, but your mind is just as locked up as Fort Knox. We become prisoners to every thought that feeds death and lies to our very existence. In fact, most people have a challenge with receiving good news or even a compliment because they've been fed lies their entire lives. This is not the life you were created to live. You have a choice.

You were created to not only live a free life, but also to be a bridge of hope for freedom to other people. How can you be a bridge for someone when you refuse to walk across your own? The walls that keep you encamped are the very walls that keep you from seeing where you are. I met men in ACJ who were freer than those walking around downtown Pittsburgh. Freedom is a state of mind that allows one to never be bound, stuck, or captive to any particular thing that has the potential of corrupting one's state of being.

As with wealth, freedom requires a state of mind in order for a state of being to exist. There is no way that one can remain free with a mind-set that is bound. In the same way, one whose state of being is free has a mind that will follow. Life exists between our thoughts and actions. Your thoughts can keep you from decisions that can change your life. In this way, you can tell what a person thinks about by simply looking at his or her actions.

I was completely unaware that I was bound. In fact, it wasn't until I received freedom that I knew what freedom really was. Of course, I was in love with God, ministry, and people, but in many ways, my mind was stuck in bondage thinking that could have kept me from experiencing the life that I have now. I can say with all honesty and sincerity that I have the best life that I could ever imagine. I wake up every morning smiling at the thought of what the day holds. Do you know what it is to wake up having no idea what the day holds but being thankful that you get another day to see what beauty awaits?

This same measure of joy, peace, and contentment can be yours. In fact, the Bible talks about our thoughts depicting who we are and what will have (Proverbs 23:7). This can be your reality; this can be your life. My life was not always this way, but I made up my mind to have all that I was created to have—no excuses. If that means I must die to my plans daily, it's worth it. In fact, I actually get excited when my plans are vetoed because I know that God is up to something.

You can also make the decision to no longer live in what was. Your present can be much better than your past. People often refer to experiences that they have had as some of the best times of their lives. However, once you accept the invitation to live a life without limits, that statement will never apply to you. Each day that follows will continue to exceed the day before, causing you to live your best life each and every day.

People often wonder how I can be so upbeat, positive, and excited about life. My response to the many questions I receive is, "Life is good, and God is great." I have no complaints, and I have a lot of things that I could choose to complain about—but what would be the point? I wouldn't be who I am without the help of the pitfalls, pit stops, eye-openers, snacks, and shortcomings along the way. I wouldn't trade my life for anything.

Strength and an ability to adapt belong to those who make a decision to learn from every lesson in life. We are too often ready to write off the pitfalls of the journey, but that's what the journey is all about. The journey is about what you went through, how you came out of it, and what you became as a result of it. Allow yourself to be exposed to the truth of all that keeps you living behind that closed-in cell. Be willing to become vulnerable before yourself and God. This is your process, by all means, but you can't do it alone.

Have you ever heard people say in reference to a bad habit that they could stop whenever they wanted? Do they usually stop the habit, or does that habit usually stop them? Most of the time, bad habits—whatever they may be—end up taking over the person's life. This happens because most people don't become aware that they have a habit until that habit has already begun ruling their lives. In this same way, we become enslaved to ourselves and limited thinking.

It is not realized until an opportunity comes along that seems too grand to be attained that one begins to feed the seed of limit. Limit functions like a fungus. You don't notice it until you've been infected. Although there are subtle indicators that something is not right, it's brushed off as a small thing—nothing to get worked up about. The indicator becomes increasingly noticeable over time, but by the time attention is given to that which has been indicated, treatment is needed.

Freedom is the treatment for the life of limit that has been indicated based on all of the signs. However, at this point, much of your life has been contaminated by limitations, ruling out surgery of any kind, calling for an entirely new life. Just as in anything in life, this will be adjustment. Living a life that you were unaware existed and is completely different from all that you know will be a process.

With this new life of freedom comes a rule book that is almost completely empty with one exception. This life of freedom is made available at the minimal cost of a simple "Yes" and will require you to never accept another offer of limit as long as you live.

# CHAPTER 22

## I Don't Want to Go to Sleep

*I will never forget the night some of my friends went out to eat. I was told that I was so tired that I had become delirious. I started laughing, crying, and yelling that I didn't want to go to sleep. My friends don't let me live down that night.*

I don't know why, but most people just won't admit when they are tired. I know that I am one to fight sleep, especially while talking on the phone. Sometimes my grandma says that I call her just to go to sleep. I really don't; it just happens. I'm awake, there's a quiet pause, I say, "Mhmm," I'm out. There was just something about that night when my friends went out to eat. It was a Friday night, which meant youth group had ended at about 11:00 p.m. They talked about going to grab a bite.

I don't recall why I was laughing hysterically, but I was. About ten minutes passed, and I was lying in my favorite spot in the living room under the chair next to the heat. I'm always cold. I told them that I was coming with them, and they said I looked a little sleepy. I refused to accept that and started putting on my shoes. What took place was bizarre and random. I told them that I was coming and not to leave without me. These were my bros (my guy friends) who often thought they were my bodyguards.

My friends told Grandma not to let me go, and that's when it began. I started laughing hysterically and telling them that I didn't want to go to sleep, Then I started crying and told them not to go without me. They looked at me, thinking, *Miracle, just got to bed. You are clearly tired.* Grandma told them, "Don't worry about her. She's delirious. Just go ahead without her." That made matters worse. I don't know what got into me that night. It was probably exhaustion.

Needless to say, I didn't go, and if I remember correctly, before they pulled off, I was knocked out. In many ways I think we should be so filled with life, joy, and excitement for what's to come that we don't want to go to sleep. On Christmas, children and many adults become anxious to see what surprises await. There is something about not knowing that excites everyone. I think it's the thrill that comes with knowing that it's going to be something good that has your name on it—signed, sealed, and delivered to you.

In the same way, life has been signed, sealed, and delivered to you. Unlike the wrapping paper we rip off of the Christmas gift, this gift of life remains sealed. We become okay with what we already have, and if we could, more than likely, we would ask for a gift receipt so that it could be returned. The thing about this gift is that if you knew what was inside, it would keep you up all night. The contents within this gift would change the meaning of joy.

Your life would become so intoxicating that you would be overwhelmed with yourself. You would try to calm down, but you wouldn't be able to. You would try to keep your composure, but it would be to no avail. You would even try to keep a straight face, but people would continually ask what happened and want to know the reason behind your smile. Your life should be so exciting and filled with the mystery and wonder of the limitless possibilities that you burst at the seams! Life should be so big that you can't even fit in it. You have so much life to live that you should look for people to extend the same offer that you received.

If this seems unlikely or impossible, chances are that your current life is pretty boring and mundane. If this life seems too good to be true, then that's a direct indicator that you have yet to open your gift.

Do so! Live a life that keeps you up all night because you are afraid you will miss something. Live a life that will make people ask if you are okay because they've never seen someone so happy. (This is a key indicator that they should be next to invite!)

I remember the day when I didn't want to go to sleep because I thought I was going to miss something. Now I have a life in which I never have to worry about missing anything because the more I live, the sweeter life becomes. Now I actually like going to sleep because I know that something amazing and beautiful waits for me that exceeds the day before.

# CHAPTER 23

## How Did It All Start?

*If there is one question that I get asked at least once a month, it is, "How did all this start?"*

In life, there are paths that we choose to take and paths that are created for us. My life has been a reflection of the latter. I don't remember ever choosing to preach or even choosing to serve God with my life. All I know is that from the very start, I had an in-depth understanding of God. Was it a gift? I would say so. When people ask me how I knew that I was called, my only response is that I believe I was born this way.

I remember being in my grandma's bedroom. I can't remember if we were watching television or just relaxing, but I do remember my grandma asking me to show her what I would do if Pastor Donald O. Clay (my pastor at the time) were to ask me to preach. My life was very different when I was a child. I grew up knowing that doctors said lots of things about me concerning my birth. I knew that my name was Miracle because only God could have kept me alive under the circumstances.

My prayer life when I was a little child was real, and I was very serious about it. For Grandma to ask me to demonstrate what I would do if I were asked to preach at the age of six was not out of the norm. I took my Bible out and preached. I also called up Pastor Clay and asked him if I could preach at church. At first, he asked, "Is this Miracle?" And then he said he would pray about it. The amazing thing about his response is that it was not quite a "No" but a "Wait." Don't be discouraged when you hear a "No," because God is preparing you for your time. During this time, I was a member of Petra International Ministries, and there were at least 1,500 members. However, at six years old, the size of the church was the least of my concerns.

About a year later, Pastor Clay called me into the sanctuary and told me that he had prayed. It was time to release to me walk out my calling. As a seven-year-old, I knew exactly what I was called to. A few months later—September, to be exact—I preached my first sermon about the man at the gate called Beautiful. From that day forward, it was apparent to everyone that this was not a game or phase that would pass; this was who I was born to be—a world-changer.

After preaching the initial time, I was given the privilege of praying with people before they entered the sanctuary. People started to line up just so that I could pray with them, so the leadership decided to just give me a microphone and have me pray before church started so that everyone could partake. At the age of thirteen, I began to travel the United States as an evangelist, and at fifteen, I started a ministry for youth in my grandma's home. Outside of preaching at a very young age, I was also very involved in two schools and was a cheerleader. I look back over those years and wonder when I slept!

I don't believe that there was anything special about me. I heard God's voice at a young age, and I decided to listen to what He said. I believe that God talks every day, but we are so distracted with our limited lives that we are unable to hear Him. We often have so much on our plates that God's voice gets drowned out by everything and everyone. A few years ago, God gave me this prayer posture model to teach people how to hear His voice.

**Prayer Posture**

1. *Get Comfortable, and Don't Rush* You can pray on your couch, the floor, anywhere—but not your bed. Some people get so

comfortable that they fall asleep. Also, do not rush. I have illustrated this teaching for about 100 people now, and we remain in prayer posture for hours. Don't get nervous; each person is different.

2. *Still Yourself, and Ask God to Remove All Distractions* Ask God, "God, remove all distractions from my day, things in my past, concerns about my to-do list for tomorrow, and any images from things seen on the television." This does not have to be your prayer. On many occasions, people will ask what they should say. This is a template. However, the important thing is that all distractions are removed. The reason this step is so important is that often, God will reveal Himself through images, words, sounds, and even feelings. But if you are distracted, you will become very confused concerning what you hear, see, or experience.

3. *Wait Patiently in Complete Silence* Each person has a different experience. However, this is what has worked for me. Throughout this book, you read a lot about God speaking to me and me obeying or hearing His voice. These three simple steps are incorporated in my prayer life quite often. Usually, God begins to speak within minutes. He has given pictures, people have experienced feelings, and some also heard His voice, which most of the time happens from within.

The ability to discern and understand the voice of God allows you to communicate with Him like never before. I go to the park with my park blanket and talk to God. I laugh, smile, and feel His presence with me on a daily basis. If at any point during prayer posture, you feel that you have lost your focus, just ask God to refocus your mind. It's okay. No one is watching. It's just you and God.

I first began to hear the voice of God as a child, and now as an adult, His voice is just as clear as the words you read on this page. This is also part of the journey. This is how it all starts.

## CHAPTER 24

# You Only Get One

*I have learned many valuable lessons in life, but one of the most important lessons of all was learning how to honor, respect, and love my parents.*

*On behalf of every person who reads this book who has parents who were not always there and struggle with the guilt and shame of decisions made, I invite you to share this chapter with them.*

One thing that my grandma taught and demonstrated for me was the importance of family. She made it clear by her actions and life that you only get one biological mother and one biological father. She instilled in me the biblical principle of honoring them for who God created them to be. There were bumps along the way; you've read about some of them. However, I have the ability to love them like Christ because He lives in me. The Bible doesn't say, "Honor your parents if they took care of you," "Honor your parents if they treated you kindly," or "Honor your parents if they came to support you." It simply says to honor them (Ephesians 6:2).

There is no clause that comes after the command that begins with "if they." In fact, it states that if you want to live a long life, this is needed. I can't express to you the journey that I've been on with my parents, but the love that I have for them is surreal. I know I don't tell them enough how proud I am of them, but Mom and Dad, I dedicate this chapter to you. In many ways, I feel your lives have inspired to me to do exactly what I'm doing now.

You both are the essence of what perseverance looks like. Sure, life has had many twists and turns, but look who's still standing. You could have given up on life, but you didn't. You could have easily thrown in the towel, but you didn't. You are here, and that tells me one thing. God invites you to life without limits. Many of your plans have already clearly been vetoed, and as a result of that, you don't have many left.

Do not spend another day looking back at who you were or even worrying about who you feel you've become, because chances are that you have believed so many lies about yourself that whatever image you have is false. Take a moment, and really think of what it looks like to finally be free and without limits. In fact, turn to the thoughts section, and write down what you want to be free from and who you want to become. Take all the time you need. Life has robbed you of freedom and the ability to dream again. I declare that your ability dream returns now.

As your daughter, I stand in the gap and believe God's very best for your lives. There are no limits to what you can do. The only limit you have, as stated in previous chapters, is what you create. Have you written your list? If so, I invite you to declare these words of empowerment.

> I have the ability to have whatever I am bold enough to pursue. I have spent enough time in my yesterdays, too much time in my tomorrows, and have never lived in the present. However, today I welcome a life without limits—a life that I have never known that has been signed, sealed, and delivered to me; a gift that until today, I've kept wrapped. At this moment, I choose to open it. I embrace where this new life will take me and believe that there will be people in my life who will help me along the

journey. I am not independent from God or people, so I will not be ashamed to ask for help. I am no longer bound to my thoughts or decisions. I am free. I am complete. I am new. I am ready to live a life that will be a reflection of eternity with God. I only get one.

# CHAPTER 25

## Happily Ever After

*Everyone gets a sweet ending
when God vetoes your plan.*

At some point in our lives, we've all wanted a happy ending. However, for most people, the reality of this becomes as realistic as being seen on the street by a producer and invited to audition for an upcoming movie. It can certainly happen, but it rarely does. In fact, most of the people who experience happily ever after don't realize it until someone tells them how good they have it. It's unfortunate, but we live in a society that very rarely sees just how blessed it really is.

For the most part, we plan, reschedule the plan, and then come up with new ideas. Life in many ways resembles this same process. We have an idea, we change the idea, and we come up with a new idea only to go back to the first. In Hollywood, the first plan would no longer exist when we went back to it, causing the scene to be dramatic. However, the amazing thing about a life without limits is the ability to create whatever you want.

There are no limits in this life. There are no guidelines to follow, and this time around, you certainly don't need to ask God to cosign. You now have access to a life that you've only imagined. The places, time, and people who are included are all based on what you allow.

Keep in mind that there aren't any limits. There is nothing too hard for God.

I asked God if He could roll everything I love to do and make it part of His plan—and He did. I am able to meet new people every day, travel, see the world, take pictures of everything, bask in His presence at the park daily, be surrounded with amazing people, share the love of Christ daily, and have a good friend who owns a cupcakery. Life gets sweeter with each new day. There are endless possibilities.

I currently live in Canada. However, by the time you read this book, there's no telling where I'll be. I could be in Brazil, Uganda, Paris, on your television screen, or maybe even married! Who knows? How exciting is that—to live each day relying on God and trusting that His plan is so much better than yours that you stop planning altogether? I absolutely love this life. It's full of surprises, and most of what you think you'll never have becomes a part of everyday living!

My goal is to always live a life that is open and exemplifies freedom. Dare to dream, and when you do, don't dream small. Go big—go really big! Your God is huge, and He wants to give you a life that blows you away—not every once in a while, but every day! I dared to dream that I would write this book in ten days! It's day four, and I am done! I am thankful to have had my plans vetoed. My daddy is the King!

The only limits you have are the ones that you create; God will veto them as well. The sky is not the limit, because if you want to skydive, you can do that, too. Live extravagantly. Live freely. Live the life you always dreamed of. Stop being worried about yesterday and anxious about tomorrow. Amazing things await you today. Everyone gets to have a sweet ending when God vetoes his or her plans! Welcome to your happily ever after.

# EPILOGUE

Many people say that life is what you make of it, but I believe that life is also what and who you allow in. You have been challenged, encouraged, and enlightened concerning the principles of limitless life. At the end of the day, the invitation is placed in your hands. You have the ability to have and become greater than anything you could imagine; the only one who can stop you is you. I challenge you to take what you've read and consider the possibility of living a life that is above and beyond anything you have ever dreamed.

It's time to live a life that people can be encouraged and uplifted by—the life you were created to have. You can either look at all of the things that have taken place and count them as losses, or you can begin to live a life of empowerment because of what you've been through. The choice is yours. There are blessings, opportunities, and people who await your arrival as you enter this new life. Don't allow yourself to stay stuck in what was. The time is now!

The best gift that you could give yourself is complete freedom. Your freedom is based on your willingness to let go of what has you bound and demonstrate your personal ability to take ownership concerning how you feel. No one can tell you what you deserve because deep down in the soul of every being, there is a sense of what he or she is created to have. Don't believe the lies of your past that kept you from moving forward. You are able to accomplish that which you are willing to pursue.

You were never created to live within the parameters of your own capabilities. Life is too big and the experiences that you deserve to have are much too vast to be limited to what you can make happen within your own power. To truly live life without limits requires you to step outside of yourself. Welcome the ideas of other people as well as their help. Surrender your plans to God, trusting that every plan that He has for you is good. Lastly, keep in mind that God has not forgotten your dreams, desires, and hopes. In fact, He is the creator of every good and perfect gift. You are a gift. Your life is a gift. Being completely free from limitations is a gift, and your desires coming into reality are gifts.

# ABOUT THE AUTHOR

Miracle Reed is a native of Pittsburgh, Pennsylvania and has been committed to serving God as well as people since 1994. It was certainly apparent from the very beginning that her life would be an inspiration to many. She was born three months premature, weighing 1.6 pounds at birth, placing her in the twentieth percentile of babies who survive weighing a little over a pound. Not only did the Great Physician take over, but He also allowed the life of one to prove to all those who would meet her that nothing is impossible with God. It is no wonder why her name is Miracle!

Under the leadership of Donald Clay, Senior Pastor of Petra International Ministries (a congregation of 1,500 at the time), Miracle delivered her first official sermon at the age of seven. This was only a small glimpse of what was to come but another indicator that a series of miraculous events would follow her life. Shortly following her first sermon, it was a known fact that Miracle was no average child but indeed called and set aside to inspire and represent God. By the age of thirteen, an extensive itinerary of ministry opportunities at various churches, group homes, correctional facilities, and colleges became her life.

When Miracle was fifteen years old, the Lord spoke to her concerning a youth ministry of her own that would take place in the home of her grandmother, where she lived. This youth ministry (Generation for Christ) was known throughout the city of Pittsburgh for four years and was featured in the *Pittsburgh Courier* and television stations for its impact in the community. Without much emphasis being given on the awards, acknowledgements, and achievements that have been received, her presence and influence are known everywhere she goes.

Miracle's parents struggled with drug addiction, and as a result, she stands tall as an advocate of hope and inspiration for people who have been challenged with this same storm. She provides and presents the way for people to see firsthand a process of freedom within the lives of her own parents. People often wonder how she managed to accomplish all that she has while experiencing great turmoil, neglect, and confusion. She often responds, "I knew from the time I was a child that I could feel alone and live in sorrow and anger or become empowered by every experience, building a bridge of hope for others while creating one for myself. I chose the latter."

Miracle's grandmother has been a guiding force in her life and gives credit to the fact that God Himself fathered Miracle, while her grandma was mother, friend, and sister. Miracle's obedience, passion, and love for God have given her the opportunities to not only preach, but also counsel and pastor not only in the United States, but also in the Caribbean and Canada, where she currently lives.

Miracle is a graduate of the Marilyn J. Davis School of the Bible, where she received her license for ministry as well as a diploma in the Bible. She is also a graduate of Geneva College, where she received bachelor degrees in both biblical studies and human services. She has created ministry discipleship programs such as Why, Me? Yes, You and Higher Ground. She recently developed $PO_2$ (People Overcoming Obstacles) and CFOA (Children and Family Of Addicts), which are initiative movements to bring forth healing, complete wholeness, family restoration, and inspiration to people around the world who have lost sight of their ability to overcome obstacles. She conducts workshops, seminars, and educational teachings that are made available through her website.

Miracle has a love for God and passion for His plan above all things. She lives each day humbled by the various opportunities to be a part of that plan. She is currently the Associate Pastor of Timbers Community Church in British Columbia, Canada, which is nothing short of an act of God. Truly, God has been faithful and out of the box, as He continues to send her to various places in the world.

Miracle believes that the only limit in life is that which we create and that one must be open to God without restraints to truly live without limits. She is living proof that there are no limits when God is in control. It is her desire to live a life that inspires others to welcome the plan of God and experience the beauty of a life that is devoted to Him.

## CONTACT MIRACLE

For more information about Miracle Reed as well as booking, go to *www.miraclereed.com*.

40 Day Devotional "Living Out Loud in a Silent World" Coming Soon

CPSIA information can be obtained at www.ICGtesting.com
Printed in the USA
LVOW06s1941030614

388447LV00001B/22/P

9 781490 816364